# The Healing Power of the Circle:

## A Collection of
## Spiritual Awakenings | 2nd Edition

### Dr. Rhonda Wells-Wilbon
Editor

### Dr. Cheryl Davenport Dozier
Co-Editor

In collaboration with the
National Association of Black Social Workers

Pearly Gates Publishing LLC
INSPIRING CHRISTIAN AUTHORS TO BE AUTHORS

Pearly Gates Publishing, LLC, Harlem, GA (USA)

The Healing Power of the Circle:
A Collection of Spiritual Awakenings | 2<sup>nd</sup> Edition

Printed in the United States of America.
Published by Pearly Gates Publishing, LLC, Harlem, GA.

In collaboration with the
National Association of Black Social Workers, Washington, DC.


Paperback ISBN 13: 978-1-948853-63-7
Hardbound ISBN 13: 978-1-948853-64-4
Library of Congress Control Number: 200892114

*The name and logo of the National Association of Black Social Workers are trademarks of the National Association of Black Social Workers.*

First Edition March 2008
Second Edition March 2023

The Healing Power of the Circle

## In Honor Of...

## Pioneer Gayle Smith *(Ancestor)*

Funding for the 2ⁿᵈ Edition of this book was made possible
by the generous donation of
**Past National President Rudolph Smith.**

Thanks also to
**Past National President Gloria Batiste-Roberts**
for making all this happen and for your continued support
of this book.

# Dedication

This book of "Spiritual Awakenings" is dedicated to everyone who embodies the National Association of Black Social Workers. Our coming together in the spirit of collective responsibility to our community for the past 40 years is an awesome testament of our courage and belief in the capacity of people of African ancestry to triumph in the face of extreme adversity.

To the Founders and Pioneer for their struggles and triumphs;

To the past Presidents who, despite challenges, produced unmistakable achievements;

To our Ancestors, Cenie "Jomo" Williams, Morris F.X. Jeff, Jr., Audrey Johnson, Karim Childs, and far too many others to call by name, yet they are all smiling;

To the Authors and Editors for their outstanding contributions to awaken our spirits;

To Black Family Development, Inc. and Alice G. Thompson, whose spirit of reciprocity helped to make publishing a reality;

And finally, but not in the least, this book is dedicated to all members and potential members. Your loyalty and efforts in helping African American children and families are the foundations on which our success is built.

*The Healing Power of the Circle* is for you.

In the spirit and joy of Harambee,

*Gloria Batiste-Roberts*, DPH, LMSW-AP
President, National Association of Black Social Workers

# National Association of Black Social Workers' Officers
## Executive Committee in 2008

| | |
|---|---|
| Dr. Gloria Batiste-Roberts | President |
| Cheikh Ahmadou Banda Mbacké | Vice-President |
| Abdul-Rahmaan Muhammand | Treasurer |
| Renata Hedrington-Jones | Recording Secretary |
| Sharon Holmes Thomas | Corresponding Secretary |
| | |
| Sharon Y. Bomar | Member-at-Large |
| John Gordon | Member-at-Large |
| Angela Benjamin | Office of Student Affairs |

### National Office Staff

| | |
|---|---|
| Dr. Sandra T. Mitchell | National Office Consultant |
| Terrence A. Bradford | National Office Manager |

**\*\*\*\*\*\*\*\*\*\***

### 2023 National Executive Board

| | |
|---|---|
| Melissa Smith Haley | President |
| Dr. Renata Hedrington-Jones | Vice-President |
| Michael "Mtumishi" Guynn | Treasurer |
| Sondera Malry | Recording Secretary |
| Damion Wilson | Corresponding Secretary |
| Catina Anderson | Member-At-Large |
| Dr. Montrell Pryor | Member-At-Large |

# Contents

## Chapter I: The Ancestors ...................................1

## Chapter II: In the Maafa .................................. 35

## Chapter III: Back In the Day,
## When We Were One ....................................... 48

# The Healing Power of the Circle

# Acknowledgments (2008)

To my husband for providing technical support that insured the format and book cover met the requirements for printing and my expectations for quality. To my sons Azaan Saalim and Jabari Jakeda for their brilliance, humor, and energy that serves as a constant reminder of why it is so important to "Be Afrikan." To my parents and grandparents who, without even knowing, raised me to exist outside the box and inside the circle.

To our President, Queen Sister Dr. Gloria Batiste-Roberts, for her vision to commission a book of spiritual awakenings for the NABSW, its family and friends, and for her graciousness in considering Cheryl and me as editors. To Katéy and Roz for their support and vision that brought forth the idea and creativity of "Spiritual Awakenings," the National Association of Black Social Workers owes you a debt of gratitude. To Sister Gladys and Baba Leonard Dunston for their total and complete support of my work with NABSW and who I am as a person. Their mentorship and guidance have been an invaluable rock in my journey to "Be Afrikan." To the Academy for African-Centered Social Work, its graduates, and the Council of Sages—particularly my mentors who are now ancestors, Drs. Morris F.X. Jeff, Jr., Miriam Ma'at- Ka-Re Monges, and Elmer P. Martin. To all the contributors whose creative energy made this a powerful volume of healing literature. To Drs. Tricia Bent-Goodley, Iris Carlton-LaNey, and Jerome Schiele for their reviews and mentorship. To my friends who contributed to this book who have no affiliation with NABSW: Ancestors Dr. Mildred McKinney and Dr. Miller Newman.

Finally, to Cheryl Dozier for her editorial eye and for tracking down contributors!

This journey has truly been a reminder of *The Healing Power of the Circle.*

# Preface (2008)

*"All that is known and all that is to be known are contained within us as we journey through life. All the knowledge, all the awareness, all the wisdom of the elders, past and yet to come, all that ever was and will ever be known, is ever about us in the realm of our creation. All that exists in the universe continuously pours forth this boundless wisdom to us. All we have to do is begin and embrace the journey."* [1]

### *Our cultural rituals are a journey.*

Inside each of us, there rests a spiritual sanctuary that connects our souls to an inner force of peace. This force allows each of us to dance to the rhythm of the drum, as we float with ease to embrace and join in the ritual of reflection and dedication that are unique to our cultural way of life. They allow us to accept the healing lore that this force of energy gives us. They restore and renew our energy in such a way that it creates within us a tranquil balance, which helps us face the challenges of our daily lives.

In a ritualistic sense, this journey awakens the spirit. For me, this journey began during an informal discussion at the Office of the New York State Division for Youth (now called the New York State Office of Children and Families) between Katéy Assem and myself. Having both been challenged by the incoming National President of the National Association of Black Social Workers, Dr. Gerald K. Smith, to serve as Co-Chairs of the National Public Policy Institute, Katéy and I quickly realized that in accepting this daunting task, we also had to come to terms with how to develop and introduce each Public Policy session as scheduled for each of the quarterly Steering Committee meetings, as well as the annual National Conference each April, in a meaningful way.

We both knew it was important to maintain an African-Centered approach and focus for each of those sessions. Within the context of the cultural experience, we knew it was paramount to develop a ritual that represented our collective beliefs and traditions. Naturally, given Katéy's primary knowledge of African rituals and traditions, it quickly became evident that prior to any further discussion on how to design and develop the Public Policy Sessions, we needed a framework for each session that allowed an opportunity for all involved to journey with us to a place where one finds their inner sanctuary that—once actualized— afforded one the opportunity to focus on the spiritual force that gives energy to our lives.

While preparing for such a journey, we knew what the elders have always taught us: While you are preparing to go on a journey, you own the journey, but after you have started, the journey owns you. With such an undertaking, we wanted the National Association of Black Social Workers to begin this journey with us. Eventually, once implemented, the organization would end up owning this, so we knew we had to choose such a journey wisely. We also realized that any outward expression of spirit is personal to each of us but can sometimes be shared when people of like minds and spirits come together. Whether spontaneous or realized, our words give honor to God and our ancestors. Our words also unleash a special bond, and, when shared in a spiritual circle, they draw energy from within each person.

Katéy and I needed to find a path for such a journey. There is an African proverb that states, "How do we go about seeking a path to our journey? An elder might respond, 'Go and ask the birds and the rocks,' or 'Go and learn from your ancestors who still walk the path.'"

We both decided to reflect for a moment on the role the elders and ancestors could have in helping us shape this journey. Almost immediately, Katéy began to share the memory of how, as a child, he would joyfully learn and join in the song his grandmother would sing as they journeyed home together each week from the marketplace. As he began his story, I noticed a spiritual transformation of his total being— one that spoke to a remembrance of a time and place which spiritually connected him with his grandmother. Even as he recalled the journey, it was evident by his physical signs that the energy the ritual created was a bond that had cemented their relationship with each other for eternity.

# The Healing Power of the Circle

So, as I listened and observed what was being revealed to me, I noticed the joy within him engulfed his entire soul and exploded with joy. In awe, I asked him to sing one of the songs he shared with his grandmother during their weekly journey together. "Pick one of your favorites—one that truly always awakens your spirit," I said. Katéy simply smiled, slowly parted his lips, and began to hum the words and tune, which began, "Oh Willow, Oh Willow." Within a few moments, he sang the song with a zeal and passion that the very foundation upon which the office stood shook. I found myself transformed to the same place he and his grandmother shared. It was precisely at that moment, late in the evening hours in July 1990, that the idea of introducing an opening ritual to frame each of the Public Policy Sessions germinated. Before Katéy finished singing, we both knew what had to follow.

It was through that epiphany that the ritual—the *Spiritual Awakening*—emerged, as it was a natural consequence of our thoughts. What was important to us was that we needed to create an opportunity for the National Association of Black Social Workers members to connect to each other with the kind of spiritual energy that bonded Katéy and his grandmother (and now me) in a healing circle of power and grace. So, as the proverbial saying goes, "The rest is history!"

At the very first Public Policy Institute Katéy and I Co-Chaired in October 1990, I am sure you have guessed by now that the first ritual was facilitated by Katéy. I am also confident that you also guessed what the very first *Spiritual Awakening* was. As the session began and we introduced the opening ritual, Katéy began to sing in the most deliberate and serene tones the song he shared with his grandmother. All present were transfixed as he shared the opening words of the song, "Oh Willow, Oh Willow."

Since that time, the National Association of Black Social Workers and many of its local chapters now include at each of its formal sessions and meetings an opening ritual called *The Spiritual Awakening*. By including the ritual as part of the journey, it has brought those present closer together. Expressions shared as *Spiritual Awakenings* have formed a single voice of gratitude, dedication, and reflection. The journey to awakening the spirit within us has given us invisibility, for it has given us the spiritual power we each need to meet each of life's challenges boldly. Indeed, it was the time shared together during the ritual of *Spiritual Awakenings* that we gained a glance at the flow and rhythm that brings past to future by being in the fullness and richness of the moment.

In the same way, those reflections of thoughts as expressed by all who followed Katéy since 1990 have their own meaning and feeling, for as each one (in their own unique way) introduced their ritual of a Spiritual Awakening, all present felt the energy. This journey will continue to flow and have no end, as the circle of power and healing endures. In the hollow of the words you will read in this book, the song of your soul will always be heard. When that happens, place this book aside and listen, for each Spiritual Awakening expressed in this book speaks to the language that travels beneath the words. It is then that you allow this time to take you on your own spiritual journey with your God, ancestors, elders, children, and community so that you are locked in the memory of spiritual grace and a bond that will ultimately unleash your own magnificent power.

**Now let this journey begin.**

Gloria Rosaline Prescod-Preudhomme, *BS, MA, MS*

---

[1] Journey to the Ancestral Self-Tamarack Song. Living in harmony With Mother Earth. Book one. Station Hill Press, 1994. Song, Tama- rack, 1948

# Foreword by Melissa Smith-Haley (2023)

Growing up in the National Association of Black Social Workers (NSBSW), I have been blessed to encounter countless dynamic Change Agents who live by the NABSW Code of Ethics and the Nguzo Saba. As Servant Leaders, we recognize:

- ❖ Umoja – Unity
- ❖ Kujichagulia – Self-Determination
- ❖ Ujima – Collective Work and Responsibility
- ❖ Ujamaa – Cooperative Economics
- ❖ Nia – Purpose
- ❖ Kuumba – Creativity
- ❖ Imani – Faith

*The Healing Power of the Circle* is a guide to liberation through utilizing faith-based spiritual practices. The Circle will never be broken. Our 5th President, Dr. Morris F.X. Jeff, Jr., taught us:

As a way of life, we follow our ancestors' model of survival from historical domestic terrorism. As we unapologetically move forward, we must embrace the spirit of Sankofa. The community is best served when we use our talents and achievements for the collective good.

The NABSW recognizes that racism and discrimination are designed to prevent self-actualization. As stated in the NABSW Code of Ethics, our responsibility is to use our skills and whole being as instruments for social change.

The Circle embodies the principles of the Nguzo Saba. We utilize our lived and learned experiences in pursuit of wellness. In doing so, we eliminate all items that separate us and remember the ties that bind us are much stronger than the hands that try to break us apart.

As we emerge in spite of epidemics, pandemics, and endemics…

WE CAN make a lasting impact on the communities we serve.

WE WILL liberate ourselves and the people we serve through our African principles and values.

WE MUST pull together in the spirit of Harambee.

It is a privilege and honor to serve as the 14th President of this mighty organization. I appreciate your commitment and look forward to a healthy and prosperous future.

**In the spirit of the Ancestors,**

*Melissa Smith-Haley*

# Foreword by Katéy Assem (2008)

This book, *The Healing Power of the Circle: A Collection of Spiritual Awakenings*, is a document for social workers, human service providers, and people who are engaged in African-centered practices. It is a book about people and community, which provides practitioners in the African Diaspora real hands-on examples and ready-to-use creative writings for beginning various rituals and ceremonies. It satisfies a hunger for a much-requested document to help African-centered people fulfill a need for a sense of purpose and connection to our common spirit. The "Awakenings"—though intended for use as opening rituals for African-centered ceremonies—extend the initial intent to cover almost all African-centered occasions.

The creativity in this book reflects the kind of commitment that all the contributors have embodied and expressed throughout their many years of membership in the National Association of Black Social Workers or associated organizations. At different stages, the book provides an opportunity for self-reflection, though it also allows one to be awakened to the philosophical and spiritual basis for African-centered social work practice as well as "just living."

Although much of the writing is in prose for ease of understanding, it also reads well as poetic renderings. Many of the contributions by the writers provide ritualistic yet simple engagement of people as they gather together in a circle for celebrations of any kind. What is especially attractive is that it offers diverse ways in which one can be African in America. As a native-born African, I find that there is an interestingly wide spectrum of African-centeredness in America, which gives all of us a new way of being African. While there are those who express their "Africanness" in their dress style only, there are also those who live "Africana" and have adopted and adapted to very traditional ways of being African in America.

So, on the one hand, there are those who find African clothing very attractive and are content with occasionally wearing their traditional African garb to church, weddings, and other functions. On the other hand, there are those who express their "Africanness" in their practices more consistently than native-born Africans. They have taken African names (sometimes confused and mixed up), but nevertheless, African! The refreshing nature of this book is that regardless of where one lives on the scale of African-centeredness, there is a place and a spiritually awakening ritual one can use on any occasion.

That is the beauty of this book. It is refreshing and serene. At times, the "Awakenings" or "Meditations" will take you to peaceful places. Other times, there is a gentle reminder of how far we still must go. No matter the space or mood it evokes, one finds strength for the difficult work that Black social and human service workers often undertake.

Being spiritually awakened by meditation is, first, a very touching and deeply personal undertaking that starts from within and then propels one to share the newly gained consciousness with others. In that regard, there is enough variety in this book to allow for connection with different people and situations. There is a meditative nature to spiritual awakenings, both for the individual reading or reciting it and for the group to which it is read or recited. You cannot awaken yourself or a community without being meditative and self-reflective. What you will find here in this book provides a wonderful opportunity for that reflection. In short, the self-reflexivity achieved through these readings can serve as a necessary precursor to communal consciousness gaining.

## The Healing Power of the Circle

I hope that each reader acquires multiple copies of this book. I recommend keeping three or four copies at a time. You must have one which you keep with you and read always. That is the one in which you make notes in the margins for yourself as you become spiritually aware and awakened by the meaning and depth of a particular "Awakening." There should be another copy that you keep in your library. Perhaps that would be the one you will have each of the contributors sign! Then, there should be one to use when you are engaging in an "Awakening" ritual. Finally, have one on hand to share with a friend or family member who needs a copy of their own.

Enjoy reading, reflecting, and sharing. Be awakened. This is your time to have a deep sense of purpose and moments in which to reflect on what it really means to be African in America.

**Omanye aba! Let happiness come. Ashe!**

*Katéy Assem*

# Introduction (2008)

*"The decision to be African is a decision about membership in and commitment to a global family. Our family is a family that carries thousands of years of history and culture, a history and culture that is second to none, a history and culture that still lives on the African continent and abroad in the Diaspora... For me to abandon African identity, even if the years have dimmed our memory of it and our perspectives about it, is to choose to abandon the fruits of the labors of our ancestors and to leave the family as our source of nurture.*
IT IS TO CHOOSE NOT TO BE, NOT TO EXIST."

### Asa Hilliard (2003) To Be Afrikan

This collection of spiritual awakenings gives substance to the experience of being a part of the Annual National Association of Black Social Workers (NABSW) Family Reunion. NABSW is a family. In 2008, we celebrated our 40th anniversary. This NABSW family has gathered each year for 40 years in communities around the country and throughout the African Diaspora to convene and discuss the critical social issues of our communities. Every year, since 1968, NABSW brings together Black social service professionals who work in the vineyards for our people. They include students, emerging professionals, seasoned professionals, noted scholars, and retired Elder warriors.

Every year, for over 40 years, Black social workers begin the Sankofa process of sitting at the feet of our Elders. These African giants are older and wiser, and they share our experiences, our expertise, and our struggles as we try to improve the conditions of our people. Every year, Black social workers sit at the feet of our brothers and sisters, hoping for answers, guidance, strategies, and solutions.

Every year, for over 40 years, we arrive from cities across America, the Caribbean, Canada, and even some from the continent of Africa. This collection of writings represents the part of us that must be "reawakened" each time we gather. Sometimes we just barely get to the conference because we are so exhausted and worn, yet we remain hungry for knowledge, affirmation, and confirmation of our labor.

The reawakening process is necessary because we are often so burdened from our jobs, families, communities, and just so tired—but we come...to be awakened to our purpose, our reason for "being" a Black social worker. We come to be revived, restored, and renewed. In the African communal tradition, we are transformed and healed. This is the process of our works' revival—the rejoining of our souls with our brothers, sisters, elders, and ancestors. This is our reawakening and reviving of our truths, power, and knowledge that rekindle our familiar hearts and spirits.

I understand this process because I, too, have come for over 25 years for those same reasons: to be inspired, energized, remotivated, validated, and supported—and to receive the hugs, nods, love, challenge of thought, and the process in which we engage. This is our opportunity to unquestionably "Just Be Afrikan." We recall that moment when we would just be able to "be still" as we listened to a "spiritual awakening" that reinforced why we needed to be "in this space, at this time, with our sisters and brothers." It gave us permission to "let go," to release, and to move forward.

This collection of "spiritual awakenings" is a tribute to our ancestors, founders, and pioneers who never forgot the collective and believed in the African worldview: "I am because we are and because we are, therefore I am." Through our awakening, we celebrate our Founder, Cenie Jomo Williams, our first National President and Executive Director whose tireless determination made sure that this organization stayed on task. It is also a tribute and thank you to our leadership, our past Presidents, our Executive Officers, and our reigning Queen President, Gloria Batiste-Roberts, whose vision for this collection is to record and pass on these jewels to our NABSW family for generations to come—"lest we forget."

This collection represents 40 years of pain and joy, sorrow and hope, determination and perseverance, along with 40 years of telling our stories and celebrating our journey. We invite you to take this collection and allow it to reawaken you, reaffirm you, prepare you for what comes next, and challenge you "To Be African."

**Harambee,**

Dr. Cheryl Davenport Dozier

Gallman, B.K.., Ani, M. & Williams, L.O. (2003). To Be Afrikan: Essays by Afrikans in the Progress of Sankofa: Returning to Our Source of Power. Maat Incorporated: Atlanta Georgia.

# The Awakening
# Hail You Mighty Pioneers

Steering Committee LA | October 2008

## Chester Marshall

Over 40 years ago, a group of Black social workers stood up for what they felt to be right, against that which they felt to be wrong. They planned and carried out a revolutionary act for the benefit of those present and the yet-unborn Black social workers. They organized themselves, blocked the doors, seized the stage, had their say, and proudly walked out in the spirit of Black liberation. Now, over 40 years later, we are reaping the harvest of their courage, bravery, selflessness, and vision. We call that harvest the *National Association of Black Social Workers!!!*

We invoke the energy of this group to help us with our current priorities. Come, Brother Jaggers! Help us join together in the spirit of Harambee. Come, Sister Better! Give us the intelligence to make wise decisions. Come, Brother Cenie! Bless us with your courageous presence. Come, Sister Coleman! Lend us your commitment to our collective struggle. Come, Brother Glasgow! Impart knowledge on us to solve our dilemmas. Come, Sister Johnson! Be a guide for us in times of struggle.

**To all our pioneers, we say thank you in the Akan tongue:**

*Medase!!! Medase!!! Medase!!!*

# NABSW

# Chapter I: The Ancestors

**NYAME NNWU NA MAWU**
**"God never dies, therefore I cannot die"** – Symbol of God's omnipresence and the perpetual existence of man's spirit.

This signifies the immortality of man's soul, believed to be a part of God. Because the soul rests with God after death, it cannot die.

The collection of spiritual awakenings in this chapter is a powerful reminder of our need to reclaim our understanding and commitment to the connection we have with our ancestors.

In full circle and awareness of the connection between the living, the living dead, and the yet unborn, we can move away from grief and celebrate again, reconnecting ourselves to those values and traditions that were so much a part of our families and communities. The act of keeping the ancestors alive through story and tradition provides purpose and daily direction in our lives, thus connecting us to our tribe and village somewhere in Africa. Where? We may never know, but not knowing doesn't keep any of us from being African and sharing those cultural values no matter where we find ourselves located in the universe.

―――――――――――――――――
*All Chapter Introductions were written by Rhonda Wells-Wilbon

In our grieving over the loss of our loved ones into the afterlife, let us not forget what Mama Marimba Ani teaches us: "All of life is preparation for what kind of ancestor we will eventually be."

So, death is not final; it is a transition into the spiritual world. It is an opportunity for us to connect with the spirits of our loved ones and find deeper meaning in the lessons and examples they gave to us. It is an opportunity for us to deepen our spiritual selves so that we are in tune enough to experience and take advantage of a new relationship with our ancestors.

It is the responsibility of those who are left behind to carry on, to pick up where others left off, and to blaze new trails—always remembering the ancestors and celebrating the past, gathering new strength from their blood that runs through our veins, teaching others of their struggles, and instilling character and brighter visions for the generations to come. We must gather ourselves, renew our commitment, and live like we know what it means to be "born again," always remembering what Baba Morris F.X. Jeff, Jr. said to us so eloquently in that thunderous voice, still resounding in the wind:

*"The Circle is Forever and Forever Never Leaves Itself and Always Returns to Itself."*

# The Opening Circle Ritual

### Dr. Morris F.X. Jeff, Jr.

Sankofahene Barima Odi Akosah

We—the village and extended family of our children—have come to form a circle to embrace our people. We open the circle to let them in so that they will know we unconditionally love them, and we are their anchor now and forever more.

We join hands in the circle for sharing and healing. The circle of life is a healing circle. In sharing our energies with each other, we serve to energize one another. Our collective energies heal all wounds and heal all that is sick in our lives. Not to share is to perish.

In its cycles, the circle allows us to redeem the mistakes of our past. In the circle, all time, space, and history are one. There is no distinction between the timeframes of the past, present, and future. They are one. This is our connection with our ancestors and the children yet unborn.

The power of life is in a circle. In the circle, energy is shared, and its power is greater than the sum of its component parts.

The womb is the first circle of life on earth for human conception.

The womb is our first circle of providence where we are absolutely provided for.

The womb is our first circle of life where we are naked and exposed, yet assured and protected.

The womb is our first circle of life where we are dependent and vulnerable and at once secured.

The womb is the first circle of life where we are attached to an order greater than I that unconditionally loves me and affirms my "we-ness." I am because we are.

The womb is our first circle of cultivation. The womb is our first circle where we are cultivated with the warm moisture of compassion, empathy, humility, and love.

When we first were born and entered this outer world of uncertainty—with all of the unpredictability—the first external circle was the family.

The family is a circle…a circle that links the past with the present and with the future.

We are surrounded by circles. The planets are circles. Earth is a circle. The stars and moon are circles. We are blessed with friendship circles.

The circle is a source of certainty.

The circle is a source of living unity.

The circle is a source of security.

The circle is the first crucible of life on earth.

Every living cell in my body is a circle. I am a temple of circles.

We join hands in a circle because all life begins in a circle, and in the original circle of life on earth (our mother's womb), we are absolutely provided for, absolutely protected, absolutely secured, and unconditionally loved.

We form the circle as a container of all possibilities in the social arena. It is a collective that is greater than its component parts.

We form the circle because the circle is God's gift of absolute unity and perfect harmony. We need absolute unity and perfect harmony in our lives today.

We form the circle because it represents all that God is: eternity. The circle is forever and forever is eternal. Forever always returns to itself and never leaves itself. This means that we will never be alone in life, isolated, or adrift without a sense of anchor.

In the circle, all that composes it is an equal distance from the center of the circle. In life, God is the center of the circle. Thus, in the circle, no matter where in the circle you find yourself, you are always at an equal distance from the Creator.

A circle is organic, penetrable, flexible, elastic, and forever expanding and constructing as it remains stable.

We form the circle as a sacred ritual to bind us with God and our ancestors whose egg and seed, blood, sweat, labor, tears, aspirations, and dreams made it possible for us to arrive thus far along the way.

We gather in the circle for the children—those born and those yet unborn—so that we may fortify them with the wisdom of our ancestors, that they may take us to the victorious shores of our destiny.

In the circle, when we keep our children surrounded, their backs are always covered. They never have to worry about danger because they always have you in a guardian and protective position.

Even the seasons form a great circle in their changing, always coming back again to where they were.

The life of a person is a circle from childhood to childhood, and so it is in everything where power moves.

The circle is the symbol and embodiment of life and humanity. It receives, gives, secures, protects, and loves those within its loving embrace. Keep the circle alive and never let it be broken.

Let not the circle be broken.

Let the circle be unbroken.

*Adapted from original papers of*
*Morris F.X. Jeff, Jr.*

# Glide Libation Ceremony

**National Association of Black Social Workers, Inc.**
**40th Anniversary Remembrance**
January 2008

## Cheikh Ahmadou Banba Mbacké

Sankofahene Barima Odi Akosah, our living-dead warrior Dr. Morris Francis Xavier Jeff, Jr., has instructed that in the African Worldview, "the circle is forever…never leaving itself, and always returning to itself."

Whenever African people come together, we form circles to reconnect and revitalize ourselves in the life-giving and life-sustaining spiritual force of the African worldview. We are spiritual people because we are an African people.

All African cultures acknowledge the continued spiritual presence of ancestors who lived and contributed to our being but have gone on before us.

Libation is a sacred communal ritual that honors ancestors who have a foot in both worlds. We ask that they join us from the North, South, East, and West as we wet the soil that produces life with the substance that sustains life.

Libation binds us to everything that now lives, has ever lived, and will live in an act of remembrance.

Today, we give honor to all those ancestors whose bravery, perseverance, and good deeds served to uplift and strengthen this mighty organization. We ask that they join us as we gather on this day of remembrance. And we say (Ashe).

Ancestors smile when they hear their names called because they know they are remembered.

In the Congo, the Lala say, "The Name is the Spirit." In Nigeria, the Ibo say, "When a person is given a name, the Spirit accepts it."

To the ancestors who gave civilization to the world and were fortunate to be buried on the soil of Alkebu-lan. We say (Ashe).

To the unknown ancestors throughout the Diaspora who suffered the cruelty of the Maafa and the Middle Passage and whose names carpet the ocean floor of Antiquity. We say (Ashe).

So that our known and beloved ancestors may also smile and know that they, too, are remembered, let us call the names aloud…

And to them, we say (Ashe).

May the collective strength and spirit of NABSW's ancestors guide us through the fear and ignorance of these times so that this mighty organization can continue its mission for another 40 years.

Let the circle be unbroken.

And in the Spirit of Harambee, we all say:

Ashe! Ashe! Ashe!

Asante Sana!

# Pouring Libation

## In the Spirit of Our Ancestory

### K. Ivy "Okolo Shadiah" Hylton

*Nyansa Bun Mu Ne Mate Masie. Orndon Nnyera Ne Fie Kwan. Asanti-Henae' Sue Ma So. Afina Sankofa Stew Gene Asum. Obi Nc hira eee, Obo-Fra Nyame. Sankofa Ghene Asum. An-Asanti-Hema.*
**Translation:** The source of wisdom is understanding. Love lights its own path; it never gets lost on its way home.

You want to know about African Spirituality? Return to your gallantry roots of ancestry—the ultimate wisdom. You do not need anyone to teach you how to get to God. Return to the ultimate wisdom: The Queen Mother Africa—the symbol of unity, enthusiasm, joy, purification of the soul…

In recognition of the spirit of the ancestors, we always pour libation in remembrance of who we are as Afrikan people before we begin a process, ceremony, or event. So, together, we will pour libation in preparation for the healing experience that this book will bring to you. Before the healing ritual begins, I ask for permission from the elders to move forward with the power of Ayare'sa (a Twi word meaning "the process of inner healing").

The elders have given permission…so let the healing begin. The preparation of the sacred ritual of pouring libation begins with prayers to the Creator and the preparation of the water for pouring. The water represents purity and the presence of the Creator. The water is also symbolic of the Middle Passage, as we remember those who lost their lives in the depth of the rolling sea, and their souls live on in the water. The water is poured into the soil or a plant that represents the soil of Mother Africa and reverence to the ancestors—the ones who came before us…the ones who gave their lives so that we may live as we do today. The bells ring to clear the space for the presence of the ancestors, and the drums roll to serve as the passageway of protection for the sacred entrance of the ritual of libation.

We call on the great Afrikan ancestors who gave their lives through the Middle Passage to the southern shores of American soil. We honor the Afrikan woman who served to keep the family together as long as she could, to survive the cruel and brutal punishments offered for just serving in the role of Queen Mother. We recognize the strength of the Afrikan man who risked his life to save his family, all while knowing he could die doing it. We bless the children who survived the trauma of witnessing the horrific murders of their mothers and fathers while being raped repeatedly by slave owners and giving birth to children they may never see, sold to the highest bidder.

It is our responsibility to research and document the validity of the **Post Slavery Trauma Disorder Phenomenon**. It is our responsibility to demonstrate the extended impact of post-traumatic experiences of being enslaved for over 400 years and the scientific connection between symptoms of trauma, grief, and the DNA of the human being.

Destined to a lifelong sentence of pain and suffering, we know pain and suffering that would later be recognized as the genetic memory of Ancestral Soul Scars. We recognize those great Afrikan leaders who lived their lives to liberate African people. We bless the lives of the descendants who have been left behind to carry on the legacy of strength, survival, and freedom for all Afrikan people.

Now, close your eyes and begin to visualize the healing taking place for all Afrikan people.

# The Healing Power of the Circle

See yourself healing and resolving all of the Trauma Soul Scars that you have deep within and allow this image to offer you a vision of wholeness right now in your feeling world. Breathe deeply…inhale to the count of five…1.2.3.4.5…and exhale to the count of five…1.2.3.4.5. Now, take two more deep breaths and then slowly open your eyes. We must first heal the Soul Scars internally so that we can experience wholeness, community, togetherness, family restoration, and love. And so, it is…Yooooooooo… Ase'.

# Ritual to Illuminate Memories of Our Ancestors

## NABSW International/Educational Conference Site Visit Dungeons, Cape Coast, Ghana, August 2007

### Gladys Sapp Dunston

LITANY:

*Leader:* We, descendants of Mother Africa, have traveled from faraway places to offer our respect and to refocus our memories of our African ancestors who were once held in bondage on these African shores and then forced to struggle through the Middle Passage into the unknown, unkind, perilous territory of western worlds.

*Response:* May we forever remember and respect our African ancestors.

*Leader:* In the spirit of SANKOFA, we seek true knowledge of our ancestors' past history of being held captive and enslaved, vowing to never allow our people to be captured and enslaved again.

*Response:* May we forever remember the past, vowing we will never again be held captive and enslaved.

*Leader:* As the mighty ocean's roar reverberates messages of their ancient, anguished moans, we remember our ancestors' struggles.

*Response:* May we forever remember the struggles of our African ancestors.

# The Healing Power of the Circle

*Leader:* The memory of afflicted women, men, and children being brutally tortured, leaving a lingering stench of spoiled lives that permeates the air, we must remember.

*Response:* May we forever remember the afflicted lives of our African ancestors.

*Leader:* Memories of wailing cries of fear, of terror, of the unknown, penetrate our consciousness as we remember the sacrifices of our African ancestors.

*Response:* May we forever remember our African ancestors' cries of fear, terror, and the unknown.

*Leader:* Wolof, Mandingo, Akan, Ewe, Yoruba, Hausa-Fulani, Ibo, and so many other traditions all bound together, yet separate, to be stripped of identity, culture, religion, and birthrights, and made to serve strangers. We must recall how our African ancestors were robbed.

*Response:* May we forever remember the theft of our African ancestors' birthrights.

*Leader:* Here we stand upon this hallowed ground, in this SANKOFA Circle of Unity and in the shadow of our African ancestors' spirits, to seek our spiritual connection with our history of whom we are as African descendants, vowing to always remember.

*Response:* May we forever remember our African connectedness.

*Leader:* With lights illuminated to pierce the darkness of our memories, we will forever be enlightened to respectfully honor and remember our African ancestors and give thanks for the Divine mercies that secure our survival. Raise your lights high and loudly declare: **SANKOFA! SANKOFA! SANKOFA! SANKOFA! SANKOFA! SANKOFA! SANKOFA!**

# Spiritual Awakening
# Los Angeles, October 2007

## Steering Committee Meeting

### David Robison

My brothers and sisters, I take great pleasure and come to you in a most humbling manner to deliver this Spiritual Awakening. You see, we are embarking upon a challenging time in this country with global ramifications, not just for African Americans, but all mankind.

As I stand before you, I must call upon our warriors watching down on us from the heavens: Cenie "Jomo," Morris "F.X.," and countless others whom we are still connected with and need their spiritual support, guidance, and direction to continue our mission to make a positive impact for our people and communities where many are left homeless and hopeless.

I can still see the visions of Cenie "Jomo" standing at the podium at a national conference, calling for a march because of the unjust treatment of hospital workers. That's the day my life was changed, and I became a radical for our people in support of NABSW.

The spiritual voices of NABSW transcend between the seriousness of Cenie "Jomo" and the rumbling beautiful sounds of Morris "F.X." calling for Harambee. They are watching and cheering us on as we work to better the conditions of our people.

The legacy of service and commitment must continue with the growth, development, leadership, and success of NABSW on the dawn of our 40th anniversary. May God help us all.

# President's Remarks:
# Funeral Services for Robert "Bob" Knox

National Association of Black Social Workers
Metropolitan Community United Methodist Church
New York, September 22, 2006

### Dr. Gloria Batiste-Roberts

We meet this morning under the shadow of a great loss. Another link in our NABSW family chain has been removed. Death is difficult and painful, but it is not the end of life. It is a part of life, the prelude to eternal life.

As we reflect on the life of Robert Knox, whom we all affectionately called "Bob," it is important to know that he was the President of the New York City Chapter of NABSW since 1985. He was an endearing and enduring figure in NABSW politics—always a fighter with a unique personality who believed in the mission and the vision of the organization and who consistently addressed issues at the heart and soul of the Black community.

Because of the qualities that made him so special and his unique style, NABSW members highly respected him and referred to Bob and his buddies—Abe Snyder, Roosevelt George, Allen Coates, Vinny Davis, Lorenzo, and others—as the "Black Mafia." I called them "The Untouchables."

But there was a great substance beyond the style, evident in the dynamic programs the New York City Chapter operates in their own building. Bob Knox did not follow a path; he blazed a trail.

# The Healing Power of the Circle

Bob had a determined spirit and the courage of a lion, never giving up…never giving in. There is an African proverb that says, "It is better to live one day as a tiger than a thousand years as a sheep."

If Bob could speak to us now, he would probably say, "This is my day! No one in the world has one exactly like it. It completes my joy. Fruitless worries are all put away, and nothing can spoil this day. I have come to the end of my journey. There is no pain in Heaven. I have proclaimed the Lord, Jesus Christ, as my personal Savior. My soul is at rest now, and my spirit is free."

Mrs. Knox, beautiful lady, please know that NABSW will not abandon you. We will continue to love you and protect you. Please be mindful of Matthew 5:4 that states, "Blessed are they who mourn, for they shall be comforted."

May God bless you.

# Collective Tribute for Our Beloved Griot, Dr. Asa G. Hilliard, III

## National Association of Black Social Workers

The National Association of Black Social Workers mourns the transition of our beloved Griot, Dr. Asa G. Hilliard, III. We will remember the scholarly lessons he taught us and continue to pass them on. He was, indeed, a giant among great men, who now takes his royal place among the ancestors. We want to share a few anecdotal expressions from our leadership regarding the void we feel and the love we shared with Baba Asa.

Gloria Batiste-Roberts, *Dr. P.H., LMSW-AP*
NABSW National President (2006-Present)

My fondest memory of the Hilliard family was their sense of family. Not only Asa, Pat, and the children, but the bond between Asa and his younger brother, Tom—one of my closest friends—who also transitioned over 20 years ago. When the Hilliard family was living in the San Francisco Bay Area, I marveled at the love the two "brothers" shared with each other and those around them. Of particular note were the expressions of humor as a significant part of our social interactions. They were two very funny fellows. I will miss Asa, just as I have missed Tom through the years.

Rudolph Smith, *MSW*
NABSW President Emeritus (1998-2002)

# The Healing Power of the Circle

Hotep Honorable Patsy Hilliard and Family,

During my 38 years as an active member of the National Association of Black Social Workers, Inc., I have enjoyed the distinct honor of working with and sharing many memorable occasions with Dr. Brother Asa. He so graciously accepted numerous invitations to attend our conferences, where he would have us sitting on the edge of our seats as he so eloquently taught us African history that we otherwise would not have received.

All of my encounters with him are fondly remembered. He was a genuine African brother who exemplified humility, patience, wisdom, and a strong passion for educating those who were seeking the African way. In essence, our world has been forever awakened by his gifts of knowledge.

**Leonard G. Dunston**, *MSW, President Emeritus (1994-1998)*
National Association of Black Social Workers, Inc.

Peace & Blessings to Sister Patsy and the entire Hilliard Family,

Dr. Asa Hilliard—known affectionately as our Brother Asa, Baba Asa, a renowned Scholar, and a Ghanian Chief—has been a true friend to NABSW and me. We are very saddened by the loss of Baba Asa Hilliard, but we can rejoice that he is among our great "living ancestors." The NABSW community knows that our own Baba Morris F.X. Jeff and Sister Miriam Maat Monges, joined by Dr. John Henrik Clark and many others, have welcomed him. Among my fondest memories were sitting at the feet of this great scholar while representing NABSW on MAAT, Inc. (Mbongi Association for Afrikan Transformation), along with other renowned scholars from our Afrikan community. May we forever stand true to the love that Baba had for each of us and the Afrikan global community. Harambee Baba Asa! May you forever live in our hearts, our minds, and our souls! Harambee, my Brother! You will be so missed—your smile, your lessons, your encouragement, your humbleness, your wisdom, and yes, your love for each of us. There are many scholars I hoped to one day meet and get to know, and I am so blessed that I had that opportunity with you. Thank you for encouraging me to write my book. I will complete it now…in your memory. To be Afrikan or not to be is the question for many! Thank you for showing us every day how *To Be Afrikan!* Asante Sana

Dr. Cheryl Davenport Dozier, *DSW*
Past Vice-President, NABSW
Chief Diversity Office, University of Georgia

Five-thousand years ago, Ptah-Hotep instructed, "If you hear those things which I have said to you, your wisdom will be fully advanced." Today, as we mourn the loss of our beloved "generous one," Baba Baffour Amankwatia, II, let us also regard his words and instruction as a means suitable for arriving at the Ma'at.

Cheikh Ahmadou Banba Mbacké, *M.S., ACSW*
NABSW National Vice President

***"We must make ourselves whole again.
We must restore and renew."***

Nana Baffour Amankwatia, II, (2003) *"To Be Afrikan"*

# Our Africanness

Cheikh Ahmadou Banba Mbacké

In the language of our ancient ancestors, I greet you in peace. Shem Hotep!

As we gather this evening in celebration, let us give thanks and praise to our most beneficent, merciful, and omnipotent Creator who makes all things possible and since the creation of humankind has been called and answered to many names.

We—Black Social Workers of African ancestry—are heart and soul, body and mind. But the very essence of our existence is our spirit…our African spirit.

What is it about us that produces the courage and the strength to overcome insurmountable odds? To survive and endure, despite unbelievable circumstances?

It is the embodiment of our Africanness—that very special essence rooted deep within us, within our history.

Beginning at the beginning in the Motherland among our ancestors, it has been passed along and handed down from generation to generation. From the hand of Ra, it was spread throughout the Diaspora, like rays of the eternal sun…touching WE, US, and I.

For eons, the Creator has heard our cries, seen our tears, and felt our pains. When we faltered or strayed, our spirits were stirred to clear a path. On May 11, 1967, one such path led to the creation of the Detroit Association of Black Social Workers.

Today, as much as in 1968, we must continue to stir that spirit as we gather to celebrate 40 years of struggle along that path to protect the Black family, Black community, and Black individual— for the very essence of our existence is the strength of our spirit…our Africanness.

Without that spirit, we are less than whole. With it, there is nothing we cannot overcome. As we have been instructed by Sankofahene Barima Odi Akosah (Dr. Morris F.X. Jeff, Jr.), our spirits are like "the circle, without beginning or end, and always returning to itself."

In the Spirit and Joy of Harambee, let us commemorate this monumental occasion as we say three times: Ashe, Ashe, Ashe!

Hotep and Asante Sana!

# They Call to Us

Janae Moore

They call to us out of the deep,
The place where yet-to-be-actualized souls gather,
Awaiting fulfillment through the efforts of those of us
Who have been blessed with opportunities
Denied to them repeatedly throughout too many lifetimes.


They call to us,
Needing us to remember their deeds and acts
As we stand taller on their shoulders
And some even carry us on their backs,
Enabling us to go places we could not now go
If they had not desired them before,
As the energies they previously expended
Are the ones now helping to move us forward,
Opening heretofore closed doors.


They call to us,
Hopeful that we will hear and heed their message
That we need not continue
To recycle the same generational pain,
Because without learning and applying the lessons,
There is nothing any of us stand to gain
If more souls keep passing on
To gather in the deep,
And their call to us to awaken
Is met only by more of us being asleep.

They call to us.
They call to us.
Let us awaken
So that we can all be actualized,
As together we realize and be our God-ordained truth,
For this is why they call to us.

# Beloved Baba Dr. Morris F.X. Jeff, Jr.

NABSW Annual Conference
Academy for African-Centered Social Work
Memorial Celebration
New Orleans, LA, April 7, 2006
(He Still Speaks to Us)

Janae Moore

He walked in the history of our culture,
Just as the history of our culture walked in him.
For when God asked the question, "Whom shall I send?"
He immediately availed himself for the task of literally going back "to fetch"
What he knew we would need in order to be free so we could again, like our ancestors,
Know "in spirit and in truth" the Thy/Thou of ourselves; the divine of ourselves; the God of ourselves.
And this is why he was, is, and always shall be *Sankofa*!

*Sankofahene* – The one who knew and understood so well the pervasive and, if left unhealed, the perpetual ramifications of our Maafa experience as an Afrikan people.

*Sankofahene* – The one who knew and understood so well that what has evolved century after century after century after centuries began as European self-hatred, insecurities, and fears, now has been rectified and projected onto us, an Afrikan people, as the most vicious and heinous acts;
Acts that have contributed to the ongoing attempt to destroy our minds, hearts, bodies, and souls;
Acts that account for the worst stories of dehumanization ever known or ever to be told to God and humankind.

And so, this is why *Sankofahene* knew and understood that the cumulative and continuing impact of these unprecedented atrocities had created such a deep and painful schism within us as well as between and amongst us,

That the depth of the distortions, disconnections, and dissonance demanded the need for something that would carry a deep, penetrating, pervasive, and perpetual vibratory resonance;

And so, before he consented to go back in order to come back yet again, he made his petition known before God, and God answered and thus gave him "the voice."

And it was with his voice that he spoke to us.

For it was his voice that allowed us to hear and receive the essence of his totality, which was Afrikan.

It was through his voice that we experienced and witnessed the purpose of his own calling, which was to assist in calling those of us still cloaked in and conditioned by the oppressor's alien and idolatrous cosmologies, theologies, philosophies, epistemologies, axiologies, and eschatologies.

For it was from all these and other falsities that he called us back to the truth of ourselves.

Because he knew and understood the mightiness of this task,
He was not afraid to make himself important to us.

Because he, like Langston, had known rivers deep and wide like the Euphrates;

# The Healing Power of the Circle

Because he, like Sterling, was a strong man who kept "a-comin' on";

Because he, like Marimba, knew to "let not the circle be broken, for the circle," as he passionately taught us, "is forever and forever, never leaves itself, and always returns unto itself";

Because he, like Jesus, was a master at working for social justice and freedom, and thus, too, like Jesus, he was a master social worker.

And this is why he used his voice and called us to Harambee.

He called us to Harambee seven times repeatedly and unceasingly, for he knew it to be a ritual of forgiveness and unity, just as he understood we must "pull together" to always overcome the enemies' tactics to divide and conquer our collective spirits— spirits which he realized could only transcend as well as ascend in harmony, peace, equality, and love...together.

And so, he used his voice to be that of a lion, roaring with an unwavering intention to wake up the consciousness of the village, for he knew our lives and the lives of our children and our children's children depended on it.

He used his voice to collect and gather the treasures of our culture and our truths, keeping them safe and guarding them sacredly until such time when we were ready to claim them as our own and thus, as ourselves.

He used his voice to speak to us and, when necessary, to hold us in the deepness of its resonation, protecting us by assuring that we did not turn around and look back until we knew what we were looking for and how to find it, lest we otherwise turn into a pillar of salt—still desiring and seeking the oppressor's images and symbols of nothingness to define and determine the essence of our beingness.

And this is why, if we lingered too long in stagnation,
His voice became like that of the cobra: hypnotic.

For he used it then to lull us into the highest state of consciousness, which he knew to be Afrikan consciousness, which he knew to be God consciousness.

For it was through his voice that we heard the voice of God,
Calling us to return home to Mother Afrika—back to the place where all life began; back past modern-day racism and oppression, past Jim Crowism and segregation, past lynchings, past rapes, past mutilations, the multitudinous horrors, and unfathomable sufferings of the plantations;

Past the Middle Passage and the putrid smells of death and desperation;

Past the dungeons the enslavers used as holding stations;

Past our first capture and our thereafter enslavement.

Back beyond the time when we were first deceived, and we then began to believe we were somehow "sinfully naked";

Back to the beginning where we were first molded in God's image, shaped into God's likeness, and, once God blew God's breath, blew God's Spirit into us; back to when we were divinely created.

For it was in the spirit of this Sankofa mission that his voice was used to speak to us.

And because he fulfilled his earthly task of returning to fetch what we needed from our past so that we can again know and thus be our truth,

God one day said, "Well done, my good and faithful servant, well done. We welcome you back home."

And because he spoke to us and taught us well,

We know his spirit—like the circle—is forever. We know his spirit—like the river—keeps right on running. We know his spirit—indomitably strong—keeps right on a-comin'.

And this is why we know that now, as an ancestor, he is still present to us, just as his call and his commitment to our cause remain the same.

And it is in this spirit—the spirit of Sankofa—that we honor and celebrate who he was, is, and always shall be.

And this is why—at this time and on this day—we say to you, our Beloved Baba Dr. Morris F.X. Jeff, Jr., *Sankofahene*.

Thank you. Thank you. Thank you for speaking to us still.

Ashe and Haraaaambbeee.

# Wake Up! Wake Up!

Denise McLane Davison

Wake up! Wake up!
Don't you hear the rhythm of our ancestors calling?
Not that continuous involvement in OPP (Other People's Problems),
But the service of Malcolm, Marcus, Moses, and Martin
Calling us to start sojourning toward the truth of today.

Wake up! Wake up!
Don't you hear the righteous calling of our ancestors?
Not to be pumped up with false egos
Drunk with the desires of this world,
But to be lifted up. Standing on the shoulders of
Mary Church, Fannie Lou, and Coretta Scott
Telling us to be like Ida and stop "idly" standing by
As our communities are engulfed in chaos and confusion.

Wake up! Wake up!
Don't you hear the rhythm of our ancestors calling us to dance Sankofa?
To remember when James declared, "To Say it Loud...I'm Black and I'm proud!"
When Curtis impressed on us to "Keep on Pushin'...Can't stop now!"
Oh, do you hear the Earth, Wind, and Fire directing us to "Keep Your Head to the Sky"?
Surely, Stevie reminded us that "Love's in Need of Love Today."
But in the true sense, we still can't help but wonder, like Marvin: "What's Goin' On?"

# The Healing Power of the Circle

Wake up! Wake up!
Don't you hear the ancestors calling us?

Calling us to service…

Calling us to justice…

Calling us to liberation…

Calling us to love…

Calling us to life…

Wake up! Wake up! *(Whispered or shouted)*

# Wisdom from the Ancestors

Empowerment vs. Evokement

Dr. Morris F.X. Jeff Jr., Sankofahene Barima Odi Aksoah

By definition, the prefix "em" means "en," which means "to provide with." Thus, em-power means to provide with power, to put into, or cover with power.

The operative word is not to empower another. From an African-centered perspective, empowerment is a false, condescending concept that is predicated on the notion that the weak and disinherited are absent of power (i.e., the moral or mental efface, the ability) to act or produce an effect upon something.

The operative word is to evoke from another that which is already within. It is an act of recalling, recollecting, remembering, surfacing, and resurfacing. It is to recreate, imaginatively. It is to educe (i.e., to draw out of and uplift the hidden, latent, or reserved assets contained within). It is to facilitate a process that brings one to the threshold of his or her own knowledge.

In the African-centered view, the weak and disinherited have contained within all of the assets of power necessary to be evoked but may lack the necessary consciousness and awareness of the power they have within. The African-Centered Social Worker's mission is to be an instrument to awaken this consciousness and evoke (not em-power) a new consciousness in those with whom we work. Evokement is the key to empowerment. When a people are awakened to the power they possess within, when this power is educed that is uplifted and evoked, they then become empowered and are capable of moving mountains. When evokement is achieved, then mountain movement day has arrived.

# A Message from the Ancestors

Dr. Elmer Martin

As you leave this monument to human tragedy and triumph, remember us—but not in anger or sorrow…

*Remember*
**We** did not struggle to keep our minds from being shackled, only to have you turn away from learning and the wise ways of the elders.

**We** did not endure bondage for you to become a slave to drugs and alcohol.

**We** did not die by the millions for you to kill one another by the thousands.

**We** did not ward off their insults and claims of our inferiority for you to hate yourself.

**We** did not become their human commodity—their black ivory, their black gold—for you to put material things over your people, even your own families and children.

**We** withstood their slaughterhouse slave ships,
Their "seasoning" and "breaking,"
For you to walk in unity and live with dignity!

# Renewal

### Dr. Mildred McKinney

Today, I realize there is no end;
There is only now, and now begins a divinely new season and
purpose in my life.

Today, I choose a new beginning
Over the pain-filled memories of the past.

Today, I choose a new season filled with purposeful thoughts and
activities.

Today, I choose to close the door to yesterday,
And open my mind, my heart, and my spirit to the blessing of this
moment.

In this moment, I am filled with Light,
I am filled with Joy,
And I am filled with Love that brings divine understanding.

For this, I am so grateful!!!

…And so, it is…

# Chapter II: In the Maafa

**AYA**

**"Fern"** - Symbol of endurance and resourcefulness.

The fern is a hardy plant that can grow in difficult places. "An individual who wears this symbol suggests that he has endured many adversities and outlasted much difficulty." (Willis, The Adinkra Dictionary)

"Mama Marimba" Dr. Marimba Ani had the wisdom to introduce us to the Kiswahili term Maafa, which literally means "disaster," to attempt to define for us, in our own words, the "Great Disaster" of the colonization and enslavement of Afrikan people. As the past Chair and Co-Chair of the National Association of Black Social Workers' National Academy for African-Centered Social Work, I and many others had the privilege and honor to sit at her feet and learn about the Maat-Maafa-Sankofa paradigm.

Maat represents wholeness and embodies the virtues of harmony, balance, justice, order, reciprocity, truth, and compassion. At our highest level of existence, We Are Maat. Because no one is able to maintain at the highest level without constant renewal, we have always had Sankofa. This teaches us to "go back and fetch It." The "It" we are seeking to return to is Maat. It is always about Maat.

But then, there was the Maafa—the "Great Disaster"—that mutilated and attempted to destroy our entire existence. It weakened us, but we were not destroyed. It took us from our homeland, but now we return. It pitted us against one another, but now we find refuge in the safety of each other's spirit of knowing. In the final days, "It cannot be defined by the Maafa. We must return our "It" to Maat." And so, It is!

# What a Strange Freedom Not to Know

*"In memory of the ancestors who lived so that I would know."*

### Dr. Rhonda Wells-Wilbon

What a strange freedom, so individual, independent, and so centered in what I need, what I want, what I have…

So centered in me, myself, and I, what I have achieved, what I have accomplished, what I think about how I feel…

What a strange freedom to not know Africa, the village, the traditions, the connection…

To not know our culture, our language, our home, our family…

To not know the sacrifice, the blood, the shackles, the death…

What a strange freedom to desire to master the way of the oppressor, internalize his way of being, thinking, viewing the world…

And all the while, turning our backs on the freedom of our ancestors.

There is no peace here or there or anywhere for us and our strange freedom…

No degree, no job, no house, no car, no bank account that will satisfy the wailings of our ancestors…

No march, no reparation, no "We Shall Overcome" song…

# NABSW

Nothing here in the Western World will return us right side up, except...

Knowing Africa, honoring her traditions, reclaiming the village, and renewing our ancestral connections.

# I Need You, God

Dr. Rhonda Wells-Wilbon

God, I Need You to Protect Me From
    Negative energy
    Harmful words
    People who give a little and take a lot
    Painful memories
    My own will when it is not in line with yours

God, I Need You to Forgive Me For
    Not always seeking Your wisdom
    The times I've chosen my own path
    When I am unable to see the light
    When my actions cause more harm than good
    Not always being on purpose

God, I Need You to Uplift Me So I Can
    Be released from heavy burdens
    Live through challenging times
    Walk by faith
    Do Your will
    Soar above it all

God, I Need You to Guide Me So I
    Take the right path
    Live on purpose
    Live without regrets
    Know where I'm going
    Can be victorious in all that I do

God, I Need You to Send Me
    Everlasting love
    Miracles every day
    People who support me
    Rays of hope and light so I can see Your way
    Peace and complete overstanding

God, I Need Your Love So That I Feel
    Beautiful and adored, even in my ugly places
    Supported in areas where I am weak
    Honored for everything I do well
    No pain from life's trials and tribulations


God, I Need You to protect me, forgive me, uplift me, guide me, send me, and love me…

So I can feel safe, start anew, be renewed, go in the right direction, get what I need, and know whose I am.

# The Great Tree

In Memory of
Dr. Morris F.X. Jeff, Jr.
Sankofahene Barima Odi Akosah

Dr. Rhonda Wells-Wilbon

A Great Tree has fallen in the Forest,
And while I was not there when it fell,
I felt the earth shake as it returned to
The source of its creation.

I heard the cries of those who had been
Nurtured by its wisdom, support, and guidance.

When I returned to the place where that Great
Tree had once stood, I expected to find a vast void.
But, instead, I found comfort in the echo
of its Mighty Voice still resounding in the wind.

I found comfort in knowing its strong branches
Had wrapped around an extended village of our
People, once lost in these Americas.

I spent time reflecting on lessons I had learned
From the Great Tree about circles, Sankofa, Ra,
& Tahuti, three in one, the seven Rs, and the
importance of rituals.

As I sat still in mourning, I remembered learning
simple lessons, just by observing the Great Tree.
These lessons I will carry with me for the rest of

my life. Such as,
Great Trees often stand alone
and you don't have to be perfect to be a Great Tree.

I learned the difference between freedom and
bondage with and without the chains, and
I learned the importance of knowing what
your work is, even when others disagree.

I learned that Great Trees move through
adversity with their heads held high, not because of
arrogance or ignorance, but because that's how
you move forward into a better space.

As I finished my reflecting and turned to depart,
Thinking surely, it would be the last time I would see
Such a Great Tree...

I looked to the earth and through my tears, I saw
Little, tiny trees blossoming all around the place
Where the Great Tree once stood.

I was reminded in that moment that Great Trees
live forever.

# Deep Within

### Dr. Rhonda Wells-Wilbon

Today, I found balance—not because I went looking for it,
But because I decided to pull it out from deep within.

I was tired of being sad, frustrated, and feeling like I had no
solution.
I was tired of not being in a good space…tired of compromising
my worldview.

So, today, I decided to open the blinds so the sun could shine
through.
I filled my home with fountains so that the healing waters could
flow.
I burned oils of lavender, green tea, citrus, and sage.
I made a list of all the things I wanted out of my life and threw it
into the fire.
And then I made another list of all those things I wanted in my life
and claimed them before God.

Today, I stopped doing all the things that made me sad or weren't
helping me grow.

Today, I found balance—not because I went out looking for it,
But because I decided to pull it out from deep within.

# What Will You Do with Me?

### Dr. Rhonda Wells-Wilbon

What will you do with me this race that I love…
> When my rhetoric seems out of line with the values we all
> use to hold?
> When I'm too young or I'm too old to fit into your plan?
> When your agenda for power and control is greater than the
> collective stand?

What will you do with me this race that I love…
> When I see the world with open eyes, no longer with
> blinders on?
> When I refuse to come along to help you chase someone
> else's dream?
> When my ultimate goal in life is no longer too mainstream?

What will you do when I appear different than you?
> Will you attempt to silence me with awful lies?
> Will you refuse communication or an opportunity to
> reconcile?
> Will you exclude me from the circle, cut off our family ties?
> Will you forget it was together that we crossed all those
> miles?
> Will you allow others to accuse me of things I have not
> done?
> Will you dishonor my contributions by teaching your
> children that my contributions were none?

What will you do with me this race that I love…
> When I boldly spread my wings and soar like a dove?
> When I refuse to buckle under and I'm still standing tall?
> When I dare to reclaim Afrika, the purpose of it all?

# We Will Survive
April 14, 2007

*Dedicated to Aunt Stephanie, Melissa, and the entire Minor Family*
*For the Readiness, Preparedness, Surviving a Disaster Conference*

## Dr. Rhonda Wells-Wilbon

We Have Survived
>Wars and rumors of wars
>Drought
>Betrayal
>Removal from our homeland

We Have Survived
>Shackles
>The Middle Passage
>The auction block
>Enslavement and colonization

We Have Survived
>Plantation life
>Picking cotton
>Lynching
>Rape and emasculation

We Have Survived
>The Underground Railroad
>The Civil War
>Migration to the North
>Separate but equal

We Have Survived
> The Brown Bag test
> Black Face
> Segregation
> Willie Lynch
> Jim Crow

We Have Survived
> Poverty
> Desegregation
> Marches
> Sit-ins
> The Civil Rights Movement

We Have Survived
> Integration
> Living in the Western World
> American Politics
> Oppression
> Modern-Day racism of every kind

And Brothers and Sisters, because we are a people of great strength, unwavering faith, and commitment to the survival of our race, with the help of our God…

### *We Will Survive*
> Broken promises
> Broken Levees
> Government neglect
> The Superdome
> The Convention Center
> Death on the streets of New Orleans
> Shotguns on the bridge into Gretna
> Separation and relocation

**We Will Survive The Maafa**

**No *one*, No *thing*** has the power to separate US from

    Our Greatness

    Our Purpose

    Our Destiny

    Our God

# Chapter III: Back In the Day, When We Were One

## BOA ME NA ME MMOA WO

**"Help me and let me help you"** – Symbol of cooperation and interdependence.

Source: *Cloth As Metaphor* by G.F. Kojo Arthur

No matter what generation you're a part of, everybody has a "back in the day." Those "good old days" represent for us all moments so clear in our memories that time for us literally stood still. The decade itself doesn't matter. What matters is this: It was our time. It was our time of being young and carefree. It was our time of family, friendship, and celebration. No matter how hard the times, it was ours! Those feelings and connections were so fresh and energizing, they shaped who we are. So, nothing in our world today can capture or quite measure up to the "good old days."

But, in our desire to recapture that time, because it was so significant to us, let us not forget that everyone has a "back in the day." These are strange times for us, but this is our children's and their children's "back in the day." This is when time stands still for us no more, but this is their time—this is the time that is shaping whom they will become.

Let us not demonize their time. It will be the same for them as our time was for us. It is written that you must train up a child in the way they must go, and they will not depart from that path. Let us celebrate their knowing…their victories. We are on the same journey. The Circle is Unbroken…Harambee!!!

# For the Record

## National Association of Black Social Workers
## 20th Anniversary Celebration Tribute

William Smart

**For the record...**
We have outlived their promises
of our demise for two decades,
And the ascending rhythm of our
survival has grown strong,
And the vitality of our commitment
has not wavered nor vanished within
the shadow of their hollow predictions.

**For the record...**
We have fought 20 years for the
struggle with perpetual allegiance—
A Black-on-Black in Black-for-Blacks
type of allegiance that still shines.
And we, the army of Black Social Workers,
still march in time with a black melody—
A life, liberty, and pursuit of happiness
melody of freedom through Harambee.

**For the record...**
Two decades of struggle have been reinforced
by a people's vision of success;
A reaffirmation of the justness of our cause.
For one day, Black children will march forth
from Black homes,
and transracial adoption will truthfully
become validated;

A triple "A" validation denoting a pathological
manifestation rooted in abstract mythology.
Ghetto houses will be devoured in flames,
and nurturing homes of pride will rise from
the ashes of neglect and shame—
Thus, visions of His will, will be done.
History will become OURstory,
which is a true story of fact.
Our righteous Code of Ethics,
combined with the sacred principles of Kwanzaa,
will become as common to the tongue
and as ingrained within our psyche as
the Pledge of Allegiance.
It will be the true Declaration of Independence.
It will come into its own psychological
moment of correctness.

**For the record...**
Twenty years of coming forth by day and night
have moved us closer toward our destiny,
And, if necessary,
we will journey for 20 more years.
For the ultimate reward is worthy
of our untiring effort—
a Cenie Williams, True Harambee, from birth to death
and beyond type of committed effort, if need be.
A warrior's effort paced in rhythmic strides,
steadily advancing in a purposeful manner.

**For the record...**
We will define the record
by empowering our manifested destiny;
a positive assertion through unity in purpose
of the oneness of action.

# The Healing Power of the Circle

**For the record…**
We, as Black Social Workers,
will help lead our people to the promised land.
We will be untouchable and unmatchable in greatness.
Freedom will be ours by any means necessary.

**For the record…**
For those who are moved by a statistical
calculation rooted in a numerical value,
WE are the record,
and our numerical value is the absolute ONE.
We will not be denied.

**For the record…**
For the struggle…
For the best that is within us…
We will be grandsationally victorious
for our people.
For the worth, virtue, and effectiveness
of the ONE—
for the love of our people,
in respect for the record,
always.

# A Word from The Creator

Nia

I wake in the morning
Searching for light,
Longing for those things that comfort me:
     A tree whose branches reach for the sky
     A flower, a bird
     The earth grounding me in my existence

I wake in the morning
Searching for peace,
Longing for the freedom that centers me in my African worldview:
     The unity shared with other African people
     African rituals, family traditions
     The ancestors calling me home to the Motherland

I wake in the morning
Searching for love,
Longing for the time when we will share the same space.

I wake…
Searching for…
Longing for…
Your touch…
Your kiss…
Your complete understanding of My Journey.

# In My Father's House – 1208

Dr. Miller Newman

In my father's house,
there are many rooms
 filled with children
 and children's children.

This compound has but two houses:
 the house of children,
 and the house of parents.
No aunts or uncles, no cousins,
no nieces or nephews—
though each, a title might bear.

Hands to hold,
voices to praise and scold,
eyes to watch and guard,
homework to check and baths to give,
meals to prepare and clothes to wash…
 everyone does a little,
 so no one does a lot.

We do not label family.
 We live it.
Every day, task by task.
Every need met
In My Father's House.

# Ohyumba Hii Niyeta

### Dr. Miller Newman

Life in a tall house
On a short street
In the big city
Full of possibilities because
Africa is our root
America is our fruit
The children—all five of them boys
Plus two-one a girl for balance
Have snatched stars from the heavens
And placed them in their eyes
So that when we look at them
We know that our ancestors have returned
To guide us
To advise us
Out of the mouths of babes my mother used to say
And so we listen for the wisdom of the elders
To guide us as we guide our progeny as they
True to our traditions
Know that we are AFRICA
And AFRICA is a place within us—
An embodiment of our spirit
And our children will guide their children
The next generation
Until we have returned from the well of souls
To guide and advise again
This house is ours.

# Chapter IV: Reclaiming a New Way

**MMERE DANE**
**"Time changes"** – Symbol of change, life's dynamics.
Source: *Cloth As Metaphor* by G.F. Kojo Arthur

We are not a people unaccustomed to change. On the contrary, we are people who have experienced a great amount of change. Some of that change, unfortunately, was imposed upon us in ways that should not have been imagined, but it is so. As a result, we sometimes dig in our heels. In these times, we are unwilling to move or consider the possibility of another way. But change is not always against us. Sometimes, change is intended to help us grow, to bring us into new levels of enlightenment.

Change, like emotional and spiritual healing, is a deliberate and necessary choice each of us must make for the benefit of us all. We must liberate ourselves, be instruments of social change for others, and hold ourselves and each other accountable. We cannot wait for reparations to move into our greatness. Yes, we are due reparations, and we should continue to fight until the crime of our colonization and enslavement is reconciled, but in the meantime, we must restore ourselves, our families, our relationships with one another, our communities, and our institutions.

We are responsible for reclaiming a new way!

# Spiritual Traffic Signals

### Spiritual Awakening
### Ribbon Cutting Ceremony
### April 2, 2007

## Joyce Washington-Ivery

THIS IS A TRAFFIC SIGNAL! Something that all of us are very familiar with. Something that, when we are late for work or an appointment, raises our anxiety when it's red. Mind you, we started out too late, and the likelihood is that we're too late to get there on time anyway. And then you have to sit there! The red light seems longer than ever. Of course, we know that the yellow light means to prepare to stop, not speed up! We tried to make it on the yellow light, but we just couldn't. After all, the police officer was sitting to our left, just waiting for us to make a move and issue a ticket. How often does it cross our minds that the light is there for our own protection, correction, and direction?

Ponder this thought. Look at this traffic light as "Spiritual Traffic Signals." The red light represents envy, pride, hatred, lust, selfishness, and irreverence. Our spirit alerts us to these hazards and cautions us to hit the brakes or risk having a serious accident.

As we move through the heavy traffic of daily living, we must be ready to respond to the "green lights" of kindness, humility, love, worship, and purity.

If we would just follow the signals found in the Scriptures, the road of life would be much easier to navigate!

LET US PRAY.

Most Gracious and Holy Father,

We come to You in the most humble way we know how. We ask for Your blessings, guidance, and direction on the leadership of this organization. We ask that You grant them the stamina they need to make the most appropriate decisions. And may those of us who are a part of their team be aware of the best way that we can assist.

We recognize that we are nothing without You. Allow us to grow professionally as we are taught new techniques to assist others. And Lord, as we navigate the "Spiritual Traffic Signals" of this life, give us the strength and foresight to allow the green lights to be a way of life for us today and forevermore.

These petitions we present to You, Amen.

# This Year, I Declare!

Janae Moore

I declare this to be the year of heightened awareness; the year of consciousness-raising to be evidenced by the actions we **will** be taking...

To assure domestic tranquility as we provide for the common defense of our right to exist without war being waged against our very being...

Because the conditioned to be unenlightened and uninformed aren't seeing, much less believing, who we are as a Godly-created people...

And thus, they—the conditioned to be unenlightened and uninformed, that is—keep on keeping centuries-old myths, stereotypes, and fallacies alive as they seek to deny and then try to hide the truth about their own inhumanity.

I declare this to be the year of peace and understanding; the year of justice for more than just those of us who have been undemocratically made into the capitalistically wealthy, the politically corrupted powerful, and the establishment elite, while too many others of us are forced to face economic, social, political, and education defeat as we are held down and back, inferiorized, and demonized...

Even as the real demons are left to keep roaming and scheming, creating dissension and division amongst all of us who actually reign from one human family.

# The Healing Power of the Circle

I declare this to be the year of speaking up; the year of not shutting up when we need to give voice to the wrongs committed against the weak, the vulnerable, the poor, and those of us who keep going mentally insane…

Because of the constantly changing rules that continuously exclude many of us from even playing, let alone staying, in this game we love to erroneously call life, where many of us are placed on the sidelines as we are made to keep getting behind the line of scrimmage as if we are not in it for the touchdown. But we are.

And this is why, in this new year, those who have been historically and untraditionally against us might as well prepare for the changes that are already occurring, as our spirits and souls can't help but to keep on stirring up and then serving up God's truth!

And this is why I emphatically declare this to be the year of liberation; the year of salvation, because deep in our souls, we already know that these treasured states come from within, and thus, no matter the multitude of sins committed against us or even by us, we are still free to be the loving, caring, forgiving, understanding, compassionate, and yes, oh indeed yes, the passionate beings God created us to be.

And for this incredible opportunity and gracious gift,
This year, I declare…

I declare sho' nuff, "We give thanks." Ashe!

# Social Work Awards Breakfast

## National Association of Black Social Workers
## March 2004

### Sondera Malry

Social Work Month is a time for us to celebrate, to be thankful, and to honor our practice and those who have served our community during this year.

As we honor our profession on this first day of March, may we all make note of its significance. Social work, indeed, is one of the most honorable, rewarding, and exalting professions worthy of **"the call"** to serve.

Will we answer the call to action after we hear the trumpet? Will each of us accept the challenge and vow to seek a higher ground as a representative of this profession? I believe we will. The Code of Ethics of NABSW speaks clearly of our commitment as both individuals and a collective community.

- ❖ We commit ourselves to the interest of our community by:
  - o Seeking to improve social conditions.
  - o Seeking to highlight the mission of advocacy over our own personal interests.
  - o Adopting the concepts of the extended family.
  - o Holding ourselves responsible for the extent of services performed.
  - o Accepting these responsibilities to protect the least of these…the disenfranchised.
  - o Standing ready to advocate with our voluntary services.

# The Healing Power of the Circle

○ Consciously using our skills and whole being as instruments for social change and action.

Our mission and vision as social workers within this community—in particular, within the Black community—is to remain cognizant of the Code and stand steadfast and ready to hear the trumpet. Be mindful, diligent, and always focused. Our clients, families, and children need our resolve.

I thank you for your presence here today in support of another Social Work Awards Breakfast. May our hearts be full of gratitude, and may we faithfully express that gratitude and be good stewards through the daily giving of our lives. May we sit together next year in greater numbers and greater commitment.

May you leave today with celebration in your heart and a willingness to continue to serve. Be proud of your profession.

Hotep & Asante Sana (Thank you)

# A Fatherless, Unprotected Boy Recalls

Dr. Morris F.X. Jeff, Jr.

I was standing alone and afraid, trembling.
I went to my father figure for protection, and he was not there
for me.
I remained alone and afraid, trembling.

I went to my mother, seeking protection, and she agreed.
From her, I learned how to protect as a woman protects—not as
a man must protect—nor did I learn to feel as men feel.
For fear of being a woman, I learned not to feel at all.

There is nothing more powerless and dangerous than a fear-filled
warrior who is numb of feeling and void of the teachings and
skills only a father-mentor can offer.

I wish I had a father-mentor man in my life…

Then, I would stop trembling so much.

# Power of The Spoken Word

Yvonne Toney

"Sticks and stones may break my bones, but words will never hurt me" was a mantra taught to many of us when we were children.

The fact of the matter is that negative words spoken against us do deeply hurt us and, at times, they can kill our spirits.

Just think about it: The unkind words we say to one another have the power of life and death, so we must use our words responsibly, especially since we have the ability to replay them repeatedly in our minds.

"Sticks and stones can break our bones, but negative words have the power to break our hearts and kill our spirits."

Be very careful what you say, how you say it, when and where you say it, and to whom you share your words.

Ashe

# Chapter V: Season of Renewal

**SANKOFA**

**"Return and get it"** – Symbol of the importance of learning from the past to build for the future.

Sankofa is a constant reminder that past experience must be a guide for the future. Learn from or build on the past. (Willis, *The Adinkra Dictionary*)

Renewal is a time for reflection and healing. Sankofa teaches us returning to the asili (source) of our power, Maat, is not optional if we value the restoration of our people.

As a people, we have much to be angry about and much to continue struggling for, but our greatest work is to heal, be whole, and be Afrikan! That is our greatest task. That is our divine purpose.

Let us not believe that it is our destiny to struggle. We have an obligation to return our people to the ways of the village that were good for our clan and the entire tribe. The season of renewal is upon us, Omanye aba! (Let happiness come!)

# Fortifying the African American Family

National Association of Black Social Workers
37th Annual Conference
New Orleans, LA, April 5-9, 2005

Spiritual Awakening / Call to the Ancestors
Opening Plenary

Tanya Quiller

Good afternoon, Brothers and Sisters. Today, I am going to share my thoughts on Fortifying the African American family. I also want to give credit to and honor our Elders, Dr. Wade Nobles and Dr. Asa Hilliard. Their articles on *To Be Afrikan* were invaluable to me as I developed this Spiritual Awakening.

According to the media, African American people are in crisis. However, we must not get lost in that assessment. Actually, the traditional African American family is the glue that holds our people together. The White European supremacy concept has attempted to destroy African American humanity through efforts to make us invisible. Dr. Nobles tells us that we are Americans by the location of our birth and by the 14th Amendment of the United States Constitution. Thus, we are both American and African and it is our African essence's dogged strength that keeps us from being torn asunder.

I believe the natural starting place for fortifying the African American family is the family, which includes related as well as non-related people. This concept of the family provides the strength that nourishes the African spirit. We can't forget that one of the strengths of the Black family and community is strong spiritual values. The family serves as a focal point to learn about our heritage. The family teaches us that "we are somebody." The family is the basis upon which we build our family.

Like Dr. Nobles, Dr. Hilliard believed the fundamental question was whether "To Be African or not To Be African." The ideology of White supremacy and its mental assault on Black people was a disabling factor for us as a race. This ideology targeted our relationships and social bonds within our families. Dr. Hilliard suggests that when we acknowledge our Africanism, we gain membership in and commitment to a global family. As families, we must claim our heritage and use it as a base for solving problems. We must put ourselves in charge of ourselves. We cannot abandon our African identity. We cannot respect others unless we love who we are. When we abandon our African identity, we abandon the fruits of the labor of our ancestors and family as our source of nurture.

The family is the core unit for our survival. From our mothers and fathers, we learn to nurture and be caregivers, as well as learn how to advocate for ourselves and others—which possibly contributes to why I chose Social Work as a career. We learn through all of our adversities that God, our families, and our mentors will be behind us and give us the strength to continue. At this point, I say that we stand and choose to be strong African Americans. However, when we stand, we must also be humble. Humbleness to our Creator helps to keep our families together.

WE ARE ALL FAMILY!!! ASHE!!!

Gallman, B.K.., Ani, M. & Williams, L.O. (2003). *To Be Afrikan: Essays by Afrikans in the Progress of Sankofa: Returning to Our Source of Power.* Maat Incorporated: Atlanta Georgia.

# Angel of Light

## Forgive Me and Make Me Whole Again

K. Ivy Hylton

Ayanna Nzinga… Angel of Light… Angel of Love…

Fill my soul with your spirit.
Make us one in the universe.
Fill my heart with your love.
Fill my mind with your light.
Oh, sweet spirit…forgive me, forgive me.
May we join again and connect with the divine cord of life.
Free me of my despair and become one with me.

Ayanna Nzinga… Free my soul for love, to love, and to be loved.

You are an ancestor in the heavens…destined to heal.
I see your light…radiant light, full as the sun's rays of life.
Forgive me… Forgive me… Forgive me,
So that I may be whole again.

Ashe

## The Declaration

And in the thoughts of the people of the collective village, they all remembered and began to visualize in their minds' eye the Purification Ritual of Life…Truth~Trust~Love & Honesty—the elements of Afrikan life. They heard the DRUMROLL and the announcement: **_"No one in the community shall absorb trauma, sadness, separation of mind and spirit alone. As long as we remember, we will be whole again."_**

# SANKOFA

K. Ivy Hylton

How did the Afrikan slave survive over 400 years of trauma, yet still we rise?

The soul songs, dances, visualizations, water rituals, herbal remedies, drums, prayers, and more saved the lives and souls of the Afrikan slave.

How did they survive millions of broken hearts and still give love?

It was the Divine Spirit that connected them to the universe that offered an unlimited capacity to love with compassion unconditionally. It was this deep love and belief in a higher power, the mystical power of the Orisha, abosum, the bio-energetic presence of life that lifted them to higher levels of consciousness.

They were able to transcend their conscious thoughts and beliefs to give life to the spirit of beingness. They knew how to use soul songs to heal the mind, body, and spirit. They understood the significance of staying close to the earth and listening to the wind.

It is our culture and belief that Afrikans are spiritual beings with a specific purpose in life, and nothing will stop this destiny.

The passion and expectation of returning "home" to the breathtaking shores of Mother Africa and the healing energy of the sun gave our ancestors hope and aspiration for freedom. Our ancestors believed that we would return to our natural place of beingness. They never gave up. They understood… SANKOFA.

# Spiritual Awakening

Rev. Dr. Glenell M. Lee-Pruitt

There is something within us that stirs a fire that keeps us fighting.

There is something within us that spurs us to go on when we want to give up.

There is something within us that speaks to our broken places and reminds us that we are sacred vessels.

There is something within us.

There is something within us that sparks our effective way of knowing what we know, just because we know.

There is something within us that rejects the thought that Europe is the teacher and Africa, the pupil.

There is something within us that lets us know we are connected by blood, by sweat, by tears to another land, another place, another people, and makes us respond to the drums of Mother Africa.

There is something within us.

There is something within us that gives us the strength to rest in our lion's den and walk in our fiery furnace.

There is something within us that our fore-parents said made them "look at their hands, and they looked new; look at their feet, and they did, too."

There is something within us that our fore-parents said "put clapping in their hands, shouting on their lips, and running in their feet."

But running to where? To do what?

They ran to fight against being strange fruits, hanging from strange trees.

They ran to fight against poll taxes, literacy tests, McCarthyism, back of the buses, low wages, no wages, and Black-only oppression.

They ran to vote.

They ran to build Tugaloo, Rust, Dillard, and Campbell Colleges—educational institutions that taught our truths to our children who learned that their truths were better than any lies others taught.

But what is that "something within us," pushing us to do in the age of "The Bush-Master," corporate corruption, inner-city renewal, displacement, school vouchers, and compassionate conservatism?

What is that "something within us" sparking us to do?

It speaks to our need to stir up the gifts within us.

It speaks to us David(s) and Davida(s) that are standing and looking into the face of the giant threatening to defeat us and take our land.

That "something within us" speaks to us to take our slingshot, smooth our rocks, hit our giants in the forehead, and watch them fall.

# The Healing Power of the Circle

That "something within us" speaks to us to acknowledge that which divides us but calls us to our collectiveness as a people.

That "something within us" calls us to unity, self-determination, cooperative economics, purpose, creativity, and faith.

That "something within us" connects us to a higher being—Jah, Yahweh, Jehovah, Allah, Elohim, God, Jesus.

It dwells in us, it holdeth the reins.

It dwells in us, it banishes pain.

It dwells in us.

It is that something like fire, shut up in our bones.

It is that something…that still, small voice.

It is that something…that spirit.

That spirit that keeps the inner person alive and thriving.

That spirit that keeps the inner person in turn with community, family, and service.

That spirit that reminds us of the importance of nonmaterial and how our souls are interdependent and interrelated with mind and body.

That spirit that reminds us of our purpose to clothe the naked—those naked who have socially been disrobed and not allowed in the cloakroom of our society.

That spirit that reminds us to feed the hungry—those hungry for the truth to be spoken to power, those hungry for liberation, revolution, revelation, and dedication.

That spirit that reminds us to visit the sick—those who are sick and tired of being sick and tired. Sick and tired of being locked up and locked out. Sick and tired of being pushed down and pushed out.

That spirit in us that reminds us to awaken from our sleep.

Work while it is day, for night cometh and no person can work.

Awaken your spirit… Stir up your gifts… Live to serve.

# May the Healing Begin

K. Ivy Hylton

African Spirituality is a creative force inspired by the Divine Presence of the God force energy of the universe.

African Spirituality is a source of Energy, Harmony, and Balance.

All human life depends upon energy in the universe. African Spirituality releases the energy necessary to create harmony and balance.

African Spirituality is kinetic energy that can move mountains, heal disease, and transform a nation of people destined for greatness.

Rituals, symbols, and prayers were methods used to obtain ancestral intervention. The ancestors are waiting for us to call on them for guidance and direction.

With a pure heart and good intentions, we can heal the Soul Scars of ancestral pain. We cannot be afraid. We must release fear, resistance, and denial.

We must rise and take charge of THE HEALING!

# A New Morn

Janae Moore

I awaken to a new morn,
And my mind immediately goes to You, God;
Conscious that You have allowed me the grace,
The sacred gift of yet another day of life.
And it is with thanksgiving in my heart
That I open myself to Your guidance, Your blessings,
Your New, as well as even deeper lessons,
Your assurances and Your protections;
Your unexpectancies and Your revelations.
And for knowing that You are masterfully orchestrating and
regulating
All that can and will happen to and for me and all others,
I begin this day grateful,
Thank You so much, Beloved God, for awakening me to a new
morn.

# Victoria Island

Dr. Miller Newman

The music has crossed continents
Our sisters sway
      hips to a beat
      drumming through our blood
Rhythms as old as Mother Earth herself
Dark and fragrant flesh and loam…one
      I see music
played on paths worn clean
by the steady moving of foot upon earth
      washed by sweat and tears
      shed before red sun
      kisses Mother Earth good morning
My sisters move from village to market
moving…moving to the rhythm
      ground nut
      banannnnnnaaaa
      black soap
      50-50 kobo…they chant
the rhythm…always the rhythm
the beat of my sisters…always
crossing the oceans…reaching…calling
      me home

# Be

## Adapted from "Before You Were Born"
## Written for Jessica Davison's Graduation Celebration
## May 26, 2007

### Denise McLane Davison

Before you were born, you entered into a contract that orchestrated the events of today.

Today sets in motion an awakening path of discovery.

Today represents a new beginning; thus, you are required to *be* present.

Stay resistant to the illusions of this world disguised as success.

Allow your true, authentic self to reign supreme.

*Be*gin with and allow all the things you know how to *be*.

Blossom into the truth of who you are.

Be peace.
Be joy.
Be strength.
Be wisdom.
Be creative.
Be wealth.
Be honor.
Be inspiration.
Be fearless.

# The Healing Power of the Circle

Be freedom.
Be integrity.
Be the opportunity.
Be the miracle.
Be the Child of The Most High God.

Know that your ancestors present 360 degrees on your behalf, creating a path that only you can walk.

The treasure box called life awaits you...

Unwrap it.

# Ode to My Medallion

**After Pablo Neruda**

Cleveland Winfield

Chaka Faye
brought me
an African
medallion
and beaded necklace
which she made herself
with her beautiful Black hands;
the continent
striped
red, gold, and green;
the beads
alternating from black
to green to gold to red.
She slipped the necklace
over my head
as though I were a
Nigerian
King
draped
in a gold
agbada
with black and green
embroidery.
Africa, your
red for bloodshed,
gold for wealth,
the green of your earth,
and black for the original

man and woman.
I was
African
for the first time
in my life.
Before, I felt
impure,
like a bastard
prince, prince
unworthy
of the gold.
Nevertheless,
I listened
to the Holy One,
Oludumare,
and kept
the Motherland
close to my heart.
I resisted
the greedy
impulse
to snatch off the necklace
and sell the beads
to a neighborhood
thrift store.
I resisted
the careless
impulse
to place it in a
shoebox and
watch it accumulate
in dust
with scratched up
Fela Kuti records,

# NABSW

dusty dashikis,
mildew-stained kufis,
toothless Black power
afro picks, and
a ripped-up poster of
John Carlos.
Like my ancestors
who raised
their babies
above their heads
toward the moon
glowing
in the night sky,
I take off my medallion,
kiss the burning colors,
and present it
to the sun.

# Savannah Winds

Corey Staten

Savanah winds blow,
Bringing to my ears a song—
A mother's love song.

Savannah grass sways,
Spirits dance as the Djembe,
The talking drum calls.

Savannah streams weave
Through the land like griots weave
Tales as old as stones.

I breathe in my past
As Africa's winds whisper
A love song to me.

# Chapter VI: Final Affirmations

**SESA WO SUBAN**
**"Change or transform your character"** – Symbol of life transformation.

This symbol combines two separate adinkra symbols: the "Morning Star," which can mean a new start to the day, placed inside the wheel, representing rotation or independent movement.

We must speak truth into existence...

We are the change for which we have been waiting...

No one and nothing can separate us from our greatness.

# An African Prayer
## (A Spiritual Awakening)

### Cheikh Ahmadou Banba Mbacké

Hear us, Almighty Creator,
Whose voice we hear in the winds of Antiquity;
Whose breath has given life to the four corners. Hear us!
We have become small and weakened by the Maafa.
We need Your strength and wisdom.

Let us walk in beauty throughout the Diaspora.
Make our eyes ever behold the red, black, and green…Africa.
Let our hands respect that which You have made.
Make our ears sharp to heed the words of the Ancient Ones.

Make us wise, Almighty Creator!
Help us understand Maat and the lessons You teach us.
Let us thrive through Sankofa and Your eternal wisdom.
Bring us into the light of Your knowledge.

We seek Umoja, Almighty Creator!
Not to be greater than our Brothers and Sisters,
But to join with them in the spirit of Harambee,
To be as one.

Bless us, Almighty Creator!
Make us always ready to come to You with clean hands and straight
eyes so that when our light fades and we sit among the ancestors,
our spirit—our Africanness—will bear no shame.

# I Affirm

Janae Moore

I affirm
that I was
created in Love
by Love, with Love
for the purpose of Love.
And because of Love,
I affirm
that I am just that:
LOVE!

# I Am, Therefore, We Are

We Are, Therefore, I Am.
**African Proverb**
**Spiritual Awakening**

**NABSW Steering Committee Meeting**
**January 11, 2003**

Denise McLane Davison

But who do they say I am?

I am singled out
I am misunderstood
I am judged
I am discriminated against
I am driving while Black
I am battered
I am bruised
I am the last hired
I am the first fired
I am underemployed
I am unemployed
I am broke
I am red-lined
I am segregated
I am exploited
I am boy
I am mammy
I am slave
I am enslaved
I am a n***** — ooooh, don't call me
    N***** — ooooh, you better watch your mouth

## NABSW

I am strange fruit
I Am, Therefore, We Are.

Who do they say we are?

We are consumers
We are impoverished
We are materialistic
We are welfare
We are home-wreckers
We are looking for a handout
We are oversexed
We are teen pregnancies
We are juvenile delinquents
We are gang-bangers
We are servants
We are high blood pressure
We are cancer: prostate and breast
We are alcoholics
We are crackheads
We are infested with HIV and AIDS
We are psychologically enslaved
We are unqualified
We are affirmative action
We are unorganized
We are crabs in a barrel
We are C.P. Time
We are mother f****** — What did you call us?!

But my Father told me I Am Divinely created in His image.

I Am that I Am.
Oh, so I Am.

# The Healing Power of the Circle

I Am Divinely Ordered
I Am the Way Maker
I Am on Purpose
I Am on a Mission
I Am a Counselor
I am an Innovator
I Am a MAN
I Am One in a Million at The March
I Am Conscience
I Am SOMEBODY
I Am the Bridge Over Troubled Waters
I Am a Pioneer
I Am Shaka Zulu
I Am Isis
I am a Visionary
I Am Womanist
I Am Nationalist
I Am Resourceful
I Am Madam President (Referencing Judith Jackson)
I Am an H.N.I.C. — Head Nubian In Charge
I Am Alpha and Omega
I Am a Virtuous Woman (Psalm 31)
I Am a Disciple of Christ
I Am an Heir to the Throne
I Am a Child of God
      His Baby Girl, Favored Son
      I Am Divinely Created!

So, because I Am, therefore, We Are.

We Are Overcome
We Are the Movement
We Are Nguzo Saba; 365 days, 24/7
We Are The 42 Principles of Maat

We Are Kings and Queens
We Are Pyramid Builders
We Are the First Civilization
We Are Power Brokers
We Are Policymakers
We Are Style Innovators
We Are Family Preservationists
We Are Lifting as We Climb
We Are Climbing Jacob's Ladder
We Are Change Agents
We Are Muddy Waters and Scott Joplin
We Are Sojourner Truth and Maxine Waters
We Are Salt-N-Pepa and Kathleen Battle
We Are the Chosen Ones
We Are To Be Afrikan
We Are the National Association of Black Social Workers
We Are Kingdom Builders!

So, Jesus once asked,
"Who do they say I am?"
I Am that I Am.
I Am; therefore, We Are.
We Are; therefore, I Am!

Ashe

# We Need Not Quit

Janelle Banks

Be encouraged, my Brothers and Sisters. The fight is not yet done.

We have been given an opportunity to make a difference in this society.

Since 1968, we—as an organization—have been fighting the good fight and uplifting the Black community through social service delivery, family preservation, youth development, advocacy, social change, and research.

We have stood in the trenches against poverty, illiteracy, oppression, and social issues.

We need not quit.

I charge you to stay steadfast in this just cause.

I charge you to use your talents and gifts to complete the things that need to be done.

I charge you to never give up on your brethren in need.

I charge you to hold tight to our vision.

I charge you to return to your communities and educate, rejuvenate, and motivate the African family.

# Glossary of Terms

1. **Agbada:** A type of flowing, wide-sleeved robe, usually decorated with embroidery, which is worn throughout much of Nigeria by important men, such as kings and chiefs, and on ceremonial occasions like weddings and funerals.
2. **Asante Sana:** Thank you.
3. **Ashe, Asé, Ashei:** Amen or so be it; it is done.
4. **Harambee:** Let's all pull together.
5. **Hotep:** Peace.
6. **Loam:** Loose, rich soil of clay and sand.
7. **Maafa:** Kiswahili for disaster; introduced by Dr. Marimba Ani to define the Great Disaster of Afrikan colonization and enslavement.
8. **Maat:** The 42 negative confessions; an ancient Egyptian guide for moral and righteous conduct.
9. **Middle Passage:** The transport of Afrikan people across the Atlantic Ocean into slavery.
10. **Oludumare:** The Nigerian word for "God."
11. **Ra:** Sun Goddess
12. **Sankofa:** Return and fetch it.

# The Editors

**Dr. Rhonda Wells-Wilbon a.k.a. "Nia"** served as the past Chair, Co-Chair, and Chief Instructor of the National Association of Black Social Workers, Academy for African-Centered Social Work and is a graduate of the 2001 Academy class. She is a proud member of the DC Metropolitan Chapter of NABSW where she has served as coordinator of the Rites of Passage program and CEU Coordinator. In her professional work, she is a tenured Associate Professor in the Department of Social Work at Morgan State University where she serves as Director of the Masters in Social Work Program, Chair of the department's Curriculum Committee, and the liaison for the Morgan Head Start Program. For the past eight years, she has been the Principle Investigator & Director of a quality childcare initiative for the District of Columbia Early Care and Education Administration where she has received over one million dollars in funding to evaluate the quality of childcare programs. Dr. Wilbon earned her Doctorate in Social Work (DSW) and MSW from the Howard University School of Social Work. She earned her Bachelor's in Social Work from Michigan State University. With over 20 years of professional social work experience, Dr. Wilbon serves as an advisor, consultant, and mentor for numerous community-based programs and initiatives.

**Dr. Cheryl Davenport Dozier** is currently the Education Consultant to the current NABSW President and previously served as a member of the Executive Committee as Vice-President and Member-at-Large. Dr. Dozier is a founding member and past officer of the Westchester Chapter and currently, she is an active member of the Greater Metro Chapter in Georgia and past Advisor of the UGA ABSW Student Chapter. She is a graduate of the Academy for African-Centered Social Work and served as a liaison to the Academy in her capacity as National Vice-President. In her professional work, she is the Associate Provost for Institutional Diversity at the University of Georgia where she also serves as a tenured Associate Professor in the School of Social Work and the Director of the Ghana Study Abroad Program. Dr. Dozier received a Doctorate in Social Welfare (DSW) from Hunter College, and an MSW from Atlanta University (now Clark Atlanta University) in Atlanta, Georgia. Dr. Dozier is an active member of many professional and civic organizations, including the Whitney M. Young, Jr. School of Social Work, National Board of Advisors at Clark Atlanta University.

# Contributors

*The Ancestors*

**Dr. Morris F.X. Jeff, Jr., Sankofahene Barima Odi Akosah** (1938-2003) was an Afrikan-Centered Social Worker. Dr. Jeff was the fifth (1986-1990) National President of the National Association of Black Social Workers. His vision and creativity led to the closing Harambee Ceremony featuring Afrikan-centered values and culture. His vision also led to the formation of the Afrikan-Centered Social Work Academy, and he served as Co-Chair from 2000 to 2003. He was a proud native of New Orleans, Louisiana, and an active member of the New Orleans NABSW Chapter, making it one of the most viable Chapters in the country. He served as Chapter President from 1978 to 1980 and was the recipient of its Founder's Award, the highest and most prestigious award given to a local chapter member. He was Director of the New Orleans Department of Human Services for 20 years. He was a dynamic voice, provocative public speaker, educator, lecturer, advocate, and activist who spoke with clarity on urban problems and solutions. In 1998, he was enstooled as Sankofahene (Chief) Barima Odi Akosah of Kibi. His mother, who was 80 at the time, witnessed the momentous occasion of which he was extremely proud.

**********

**Dr. Elmer P. Martin** (1946-2001) was an active member of the National Association of Black Social Workers and a member of the Council of Sages for the Academy for African-Centered Social Work. Dr. Martin was the Co-Founder and Executive Director of the National Black Experience-Based Social Work Institute and President and Founder of The Great Blacks in Wax Museum, Inc. in Baltimore Maryland. He was a tenured full Professor in the

Department of Social Work and Mental Health at Morgan State University for over 25 years. He co-authored four books with his wife, Dr. Joanne M. Martin: *Social Work and the Black Experience, The Healing Tradition in The Black Family and Community, The Black Extended Family,* and *Spirituality and the Black Helping Tradition.*

\*\*\*\*\*\*\*\*\*\*

**Dr. Mildred McKinney** (1935-2005) was a spiritual guide and mentor for many students, faculty, and staff at Morgan State University for over 31 years where she was on faculty in the Department of Social Work and served as an advisor and confidant for the football team, University Choir, Honda Academic All-Star Challenge Team, and coordinated the University Coronation which crowned Mr. & Mrs. Morgan. She was an African-centered educator and served as a spiritual guide for Dr. Wells-Wilbon and countless others.

# The Creative Energy Force

**Dr. Gloria Batiste-Roberts** is the 10th National President of the National Association of Black Social Workers. She is the immediate past President of the Houston Chapter of NABSW; Vice-President of the National Black Child Development Institute, Houston Chapter; and a life member of the National Association for the Advancement of Colored People. Dr. Batiste-Roberts received her BSW from Texas Southern University, her MSW from Howard University, and a Doctorate in Public Health from the University of Texas School of Public Health. For 29 ½ years, she worked for the Texas Department of Family and Protective Services as a supervisor, and for 21 years, she worked part-time as an Emergency Room Social Worker at Ben Tab Hospital. For the past 32 years, she has served as Assistant Debate Coach at Texas Southern University, Director of the Annual Barbara Jordan Memorial lecture, the Thomas F. Freeman Intramural Forensic Festival, and the Thomas F. Freeman Smooth Talkers Tournament for middle school students. She also serves as a Permanency Convener for Children's Protective Services and Adjunct Professor in the School of Social Work at Texas Southern University.

\*\*\*\*\*\*\*\*\*\*

**Janelle B. Banks** served as Secretary of the ABSW Chapter at the University of Georgia. She also served as Parliamentarian and Second Vice-President of the NABSW Office of Student Affairs. She lives in Ellenwood, Georgia, with her husband, Joseph E. Banks, Jr., and daughter, Janaé Marie. Mrs. Banks is a Special Education Teacher at North Clayton High School. She is a graduate of South Carolina State University and took Master's-level courses in Social Work at the University of Georgia. She is a member of Alpha Kappa Alpha Sorority, Inc.

# NABSW

**********

**Gladys S. Dunston** is a retired School Social Worker who practiced in the field of Social Work for over 35 years. She has been an active member of the NABSW since 1969 when she joined the New York City Chapter. Other Chapter affiliations include Triangle ABSW, Albany, New York, and Westchester ABSW where she served in the capacity of Chapter President and one of the founding Elders of the Female Rites of Passage Project. She is a graduate of the NABSW National Academy for African-Centered Social Work. Mrs. Dunston, fondly known as "Mama Gladys," is currently an active member of TABSW and serves as Co-Chair of the Sankofa Mentorship Project. She is the wife of NABSW National Past President, Baba Leonard G. Dunston, and mother to Kioka and Kwame, as well as many others.

**********

**K. Ivy Hylton** is a practicing Licensed Independent Clinical Social Worker, Wellness Consultant, Consumer Advocate, Professional Development Trainer, and Organizational Development Specialist. Ms. Hylton serves on the Council of Sages for the National Association of Black Social Workers African-Centered Social Work Academy. With over 28 years of diversified experience, Ms. Hylton is now the Vice-President and Clinical Director for Youth and Families in Crisis, LLC—a family-based consulting firm offering innovative concepts in family strengthening, youth diversion, reentry restorative justice programs, and personal transformation.

**********

**Rev. Dr. Glenell M. Lee-Pruitt** is the Pastor of Solomon Chapel African Methodist Episcopal Church in Cleveland, Mississippi. She is also the Dean of University College and Assistant Professor of Social Work at Mississippi Valley State University in Itta Bena, Mississippi.

**********

**Sondera Malry** is a Clinical Supervisor with the Department of Family and Protective Services (DFPS), specializing in the Strengthening Families Initiative Project (SFI). She has been a dedicated and loyal member of the Houston, Texas Chapter of NABSW for more than 26 years. She completed her undergraduate degree at Louisiana State University in Sociology. She obtained her MSW from the University of Houston, specializing in Planning and Administration. She is a Licensed Advanced Clinical Practitioner for the State of Texas.

**********

**Denise McLane-Davison**, MSW, joined the NABSW family as a second year MSW student at the University of Chicago through the Chicago Chapter in 1987. She served as founding Faculty Advisor for the Illinois State University Student Chapter (1993 to 2000); Faculty Advisor for the Office of Student Affairs (1999 to 2002); Co-Chair of the AIDS Task Force (1998 to 2002); and Faculty Advisor, University of Georgia Chapter (2006 to present). Ms. Davison is a proud graduate of the 2000 class of the Academy for African-Centered Social Work. She is currently the Coordinator of Field Education at the University of Georgia School of Social Work and is completing her Ph.D. at the Whitney M. Young School of Social Work, Clark Atlanta University.

**********

# NABSW

**Chester Marshall** has been a member of the National Association of Black Social Workers for 21 years. He is a member of the DC Metropolitan Chapter, a graduate of the Academy for African-Centered Social Work, and is currently the Co-Chair of the National NABSW Public Policy Committee. Mr. Marshall is the Founder and CEO of the Institute for African Man Development in Washington, DC. The Institute is a 501(c)3 organization that specializes in the provision of social services for African American Men and Boys.

\*\*\*\*\*\*\*\*\*\*

**Janae Moore** is a Licensed Clinical Social Worker, a member of the DC Metro Chapter of NABSW, and a graduate of the Academy for African-Centered Social Work. She is the Founder and Operator of Taranga House Retreat & Practice Center where she seeks to utilize her gifts and skills of hospitality, counseling, and writing to love and serve others. Janae is currently pursuing a Doctor of Ministry degree at United Theological Seminary in Trotwood, Ohio, and is employed to provide hospice care, support, and services to persons with life-limiting illnesses and their families in Northern Virginia. She resides in Accokeek, Maryland, and is the mother of two young adult males, Jalon and Darell.

\*\*\*\*\*\*\*\*\*\*

**Dr. Miller Newman** lives in Washington, DC, with her husband, David Gadson, and in the African-centered tradition, a huge extended family of fictive and non-fictive kinship. Dr. Newman teaches English Composition at Montgomery College in Rockville, Maryland. She writes poetry and prose and is currently working on her first novel.

\*\*\*\*\*\*\*\*\*\*

**David Robison** is President of the Dallas Chapter of NABSW. He was first affiliated with NABSW in 1979 as an employee of the West Dallas Community Centers, Inc., a youth service agency. He has a B.A. in Political Science, with a concentration in Social Work from the University of Texas at Arlington. He is currently an MBA student at the University of Phoenix. Professional experiences include Administrative Manager, City of Dallas for 12 years, and District Parole Officer, Texas Department of Criminal Justice for 20 years. He currently serves as Director and Consultant for Proactive Approaches to Community Supervision (PACS); Community Resource One Stop Systems (CROSS) Reentry Program; and Principal for CAD Global Marketing Group.

*********

**William Smart** is a member of the Chicago Chapter of NABSW and wrote "For the Record" in celebration of our 20th anniversary.

*********

**Corey Staten** is a 2003 Summa Cum Laude graduate of Old Dominion University in Norfolk, Virginia. Despite being totally blind since the age of 19, he is an accomplished playwright and performing artist. He has written and produced the stage play, "Roots of the Withered Tree," which ran in 2002 and 2004. Since 2001, he has performed nationally as a musician and as the featured griot with Atumpan: The Talking Drums. He currently resides in Virginia's Hampton Roads Region, utilizing his talents as a Museum Education Specialist with his wife, Marie, and their one-year-old daughter, Brooklyn.

*********

**Tanya Quiller** is a graduate of Texas Southern University with a Bachelor's in Social Work. She will receive an M.A. in Counseling from Prairie View A&M University. She is a member of the National Association of Social Workers, the National Association of Black Social Workers of Texas, and Chi Sigma Iota, Epsilon Chapter. She is a member of Greater Vision Church where she is the Assistant Director of the Women of the Word (WOW) Ministry and Daughters of Esther ministry, a Youth Matron, a Youth Sunday School Teacher, a Youth Christian Enrichment Studies Teacher, Hospitality Ministry, and the choir. Tanya is currently employed by the Department of Family and Protective Services.

**\*\*\*\*\*\*\*\*\***

**Yvonne Toney** is a proud member of the Houston Chapter of NABSW and has provided aerobic classes at the National Conference for the past several years. She was born and raised in Brooklyn, New York, and moved to Houston, Texas at the age of 18. Ms. Toney has worked with the Harris County Hospital District as a Secretary, Office Manager, and now, Coordinator. Her main priority in life is to be a blessing to everyone she comes in contact with and be an instrument of the Creator.

**\*\*\*\*\*\*\*\*\***

# The Healing Power of the Circle

**Joyce Washington Ivery** has been an active member of the National Association of Black Social Workers for nearly 40 years during which time she has been an active member of the New Orleans Chapter and served as an Officer. She has served as an active member of the Conference Committee – Registration Committee Chairperson from 1986 to 1998, and Exhibit Chairperson from 1998 to 2007. She is originally from New Orleans, Louisiana, but relocated to Natchez, Mississippi following the devastation of her home during Hurricane Katrina. In Natchez, she was reunited with the maternal side of her family.

**********

**Cleveland Winfield** teaches 10th-grade English, Creative Writing, and African American Studies at Rappahannock High School in Warsaw, Virginia. He serves as an Adjunct Professor of English Composition and an Upward Bound Instructor for Rappahannock Community College. As an aspiring artist and devout proponent of Hip-Hop culture, he founded the *Elemental Renaissance*—a Virginia Hip-Hop publication at Old Dominion University on September 25, 1999.

# NABSW

# Personal Healing Notes

_____

_____

_____

_____

_____

_____

_____

_____

_____

_____

_____

_____

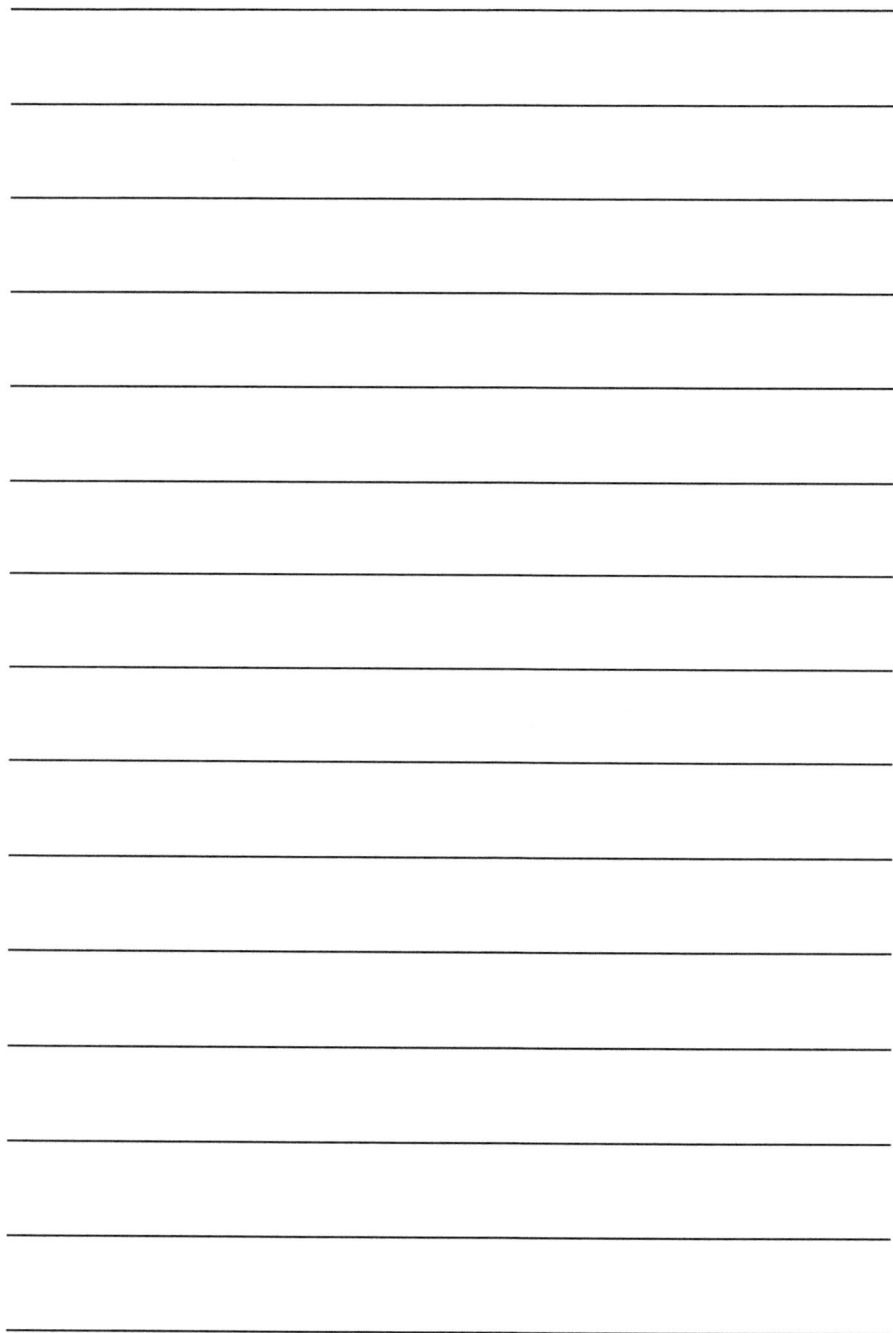

www.ingramcontent.com/pod-product-compliance
Lightning Source LLC
Chambersburg PA
CBHW060436090426
42733CB00011B/2293